Purple Robert

Volume 01

'Mrs. Sharwood is My Concubine'

Edition 01-Revision 13

Purple Robert

Volume 01

'Mrs. Sharwood is My Concubine'

All current
Contact & Sales Information
Can be found at
www.PurpleRobert.com

Purple Robert

Volume 01

'Mrs. Sharwood is My Concubine'

ISBN Number 978-1-910686-88-1

First published

December 2015 by Whispering Word

All current contact and sales information can be found at

www.PurpleRobert.com

Printed in The United Kingdom

for

WhisperingWord

Purple Robert

Volume 01

'Mrs. Sharwood is My Concubine'

Dedication

This book is dedicated, very simply,

To the now four most important people

In the whole wide world to me.

My daughter Gemma,

My son Jonathan,

My grandaughter Ellie May,

And of course,

My wife

Bridget.

Grammar, Bible Versions & WARNINGS!

To be British, is to be somewhat like 'the last of the Mohicans.' The Britain, that is, the United Kingdom I grew up in is breaking apart. No, sadly, it is broken and never to be repaired. Even so, I am of Irish & Scottish great-grandparents, grandparents and parents, and I was also born in England. Therefore, I am British and a Celt at that. In addition to this, I love North America and the South in particular, so much so, that I feel like a British Red-Neck. Does this make me a Yankophile, or loving the South in particular (and its battle flag) does it make me more especially a Dixiophile? Alternatively, maybe I could be an Americophile or a Canameriphile? Who knows? Suffice to say, that as our nations were once only divided by a common 'English' language, (America still being the residence of the majority of our English readers,) I have tried to adopt the spelling and grammar of the Americas. In this, I have no doubt failed, and in the so doing, both mixed and matched the UK and US spelling and English grammatical styles. In doing this, I confess that I am a double-minded man, and unstable in all my editorial ways. The purists, either side of the pond, I am sure will never forgive me. The rest do not care. Either way, I need your help. So, if you spot any 'howlers,' do let me know. Email me your corrections on,

getyouracttogetherman@whisperingword.com

BIBLE VERSIONS

Ah, the Bible. The true meta-narrative of the real world and therefore all things meta-physical. Well, preferring the 'Textus Receptus' or the 'Majority Text,' I have tried to use the New Separatist Bible (NSB), which is a confluence Bible based on the 1560 Geneva Bible and the 1611 Authorized version, (Pure Cambridge Edition) when I have referenced the Bible, though where necessary, for mere contemporary clarity of course, when I have I have deviated from this norm, at that time I have clearly indicated which other Bible Version has been referenced.

SIX FIRST WARNINGS!

If you are easily offended by low level expletives...**Go no further. Do not read this book!** If you are prudish in any way ...**Go no further. Do not read this book!** If you do not want to be challenged...**Go no further. Do not read this book!** If you want to be stroked into unhindered sleep and into the stupor of remaining as you are...**Go no further. Do not read this book!** If you hide under the respectable covers of a comfortable religion...**Go no**

further. Do not read this book! If you are frail in faith and dishonest about life under this sun…**Go no further. Do not read this book!** If you have no real integrity regarding the state of your own heart…. **Go no further. Do not read this book!** If however, you are grown up, honest and have a basic human integrity, **ENJOY!**

Just a Huckster

Some young preacher will study until he has to get thick glasses to take care of his failing eyesight because he has an idea he wants to become a famous preacher. HE'S JUST A HUCKSTER buying selling and getting gain. They will ordain him and he will be known as Reverend and if he writes a book, they will make him a doctor. And he will be known as Doctor; but he's still a huckster buying and selling and getting gain.

And when the Lord comes back,
HE will drive him out of the temple
along with the other cattle.

A.W. Tozer

(from 'Tozer on Christian Leadership,' compiled by Ron Eggert)

John 3:30 He must increase
but I must decrease.

Preface

I want you to 'experience' these 66 poetic 'devotions,' and to that end, there is little I will speak of that I have not actually experienced myself. Indeed, in those areas where I have lacked such experience, I have by night and by day, tried to extend my mind and soul into them, even burgling these experiences from other men's minds, sniffing the air of their spirit whilst noting the position and habitation of these experiential treasures of other people, looking, listening and finally gathering them to my chest, often just before very quickly getting out of their houses before I am discovered. When necessary, after returning from some of these 'night-time' reconnoitres, I have had to burn the un-cleanable, infected and incriminating clothes of my own soul lest I become infiltrated by the darkness of some of the burgled and bad consequences carried from them and so come under the accusation of him who always stands against me. (Rev 12:10).

My 'daytime' intrusions into unknown and lighter experiences, have however, overall been pleasant, and the memory of them has lingered, and nicely so. On some occasions, when I have been discovered burgling the houses of other people's minds and emotions in the day, I have been given a trophy to take with me, and an invitation, even an expectation to return another bright day and look a little closer, stay a little longer. People like to share their nice experiences.

These poems then, through some are both burgled and borrowed, most are the expressive experiences of my heart from both the days and nights of my own soul. Remember though please, that poetry is essentially the communication of the heart, of experience, and so I want you to also experience these poetic observations and to that end, as I have said, there is little I will speak of that I have not actually experienced, or expect or hope to experience myself. This is important.

I also believe that poets speak porously, leaving behind a personal and adaptive language that keeps on telling, and often talks louder, longer, and with a consuming clarity on the power wave of the listeners own reflections. Poetry seeps and spreads, you see, for when that noise of the spoken words grow ever louder and clearer, the poet's voice has then become the listener's voice, because the listener's voice will now have consumed the words, now have begun owning the piece or pieces of the poem for themselves. So, what is now become their poem will have open and become a portal to the discovery of their own deep places where they realize, that actually, a million others already dwell there in the dark along with them, and maybe even God, for I think maybe God inspects the labyrinths of our larynx's and if He likes them, He then inhabits them (Psalm 22:3). You see, poetry, speaks and keeps on uttering. Poetry discovers you. Poetry is God disclosing you to yourself and on a good day, through it, He might even reveal some of Himself and His desire toward you. To these ends of utterance, this is an experiential devotional book of metaphysical poetry. On the other hand, maybe it is just me droning on.

I consider myself to be contrary to Keats in that I am a 'Biblical Metaphysical Realist' embracing mysteries whilst continuing to ask questions, both whilst being dragged kicking and screaming through hell, as well as refusing to sit quietly whilst being bussed through beauty and surrounded by wonders. In any event, death always makes Metaphysical Biblical Realism, didactic, for it is more than common sense clothed in questions, yes, it is Biblical Metaphysical Reality! A scary shout from the slick black side of a six foot grave, all decked in diamonds and cumbered about by dry black cancer.

Please note as well then, that these poems are mostly fitted for performance and best heard when read aloud. Therefore, where appropriate I have also given some performance instructions. In the end though, I say again that I do hope that whilst recognizing my voice, that these poems also become a carrier wave for your very own and very distinct voice yet to be discovered by you. This is my deep desire for you. So, read the pieces aloud for yourself and make them your very own! Fully put yourself in them.

Lastly, despite this being a book of personal experiential devotional pieces, all my gathered experiences, discoveries and observations are still under question. They are questionable. Therefore, I also try to bring them under the discovering light of God's Word each day as well. Could I also ask you to consider that when God communicates in prose, He communicates His mind, but when God communicates in Poetry, He communicates his heart. I too am communicating my own heart's experiences and with purpose! That purpose is to connect with your own hearts feelings and to ignite your imagination, and thereby, to sharpen the perception of your own metaphysical awareness, as well as to communicate sound Biblical teaching, ranging from ethics to basic Christian doctrine, all of which, I hope, will affect how you practice life.

Bearing all this in mind then, I am sure that you will find this book to be full of pressed flowers as well as old seaweed. Such is life under this present sun. In the openness of each piece, in its attempted honesty, I do pray very much that you will discover more of the reality of the touchable God and of the solidness of who you truly are, and if you are a Christian, then of who you truly are in Him. .

Finally, for those who think with their feelings, I do hope this book makes you feel and therefore think deeply, and also then makes you begin speaking honest and right words into the ever-open ears of God the great who is also God the good.

Purple Robert June 2019, Scotland

'PEPTEN' and Permissions

Each of these 66 poems are followed by a **P**reamble, **E**xplanation, **P**erformance **T**ips and **E**nd **N**otes. I have put these at the end of each piece because I don't want them to initially distract you from your own reading of the poem. Therefore, as a brief word of explanation, at the end of each piece you will find a,

PREAMBLE

This will usually be a verse or verses from God's Holy Word, the Bible, and the New Separatist Bible (NSB) in particular.

EXPLANATION

This will reveal some of the poetic-drivers, ignition points and intentions of the poem.

PERFORMANCE TIPS

Yes indeed, poetry is for the stage rather than the page. So, to give you some encouragement to perform the piece, even for yourself, I give you some tips of my original intentions regarding communication of the same.

END NOTES

Sometimes the 'End Notes' are lengthier than the poems! In an age of vast Biblical ignorance (and that's just in the church) without these end-notes, the nuances and obvious references to the Scriptures intimated at contained in the poems would be missed. Being a Biblical Metaphysical Realist, I am also excited to put these Bible-Links there, for the Bible is, indeed, the most exciting book in the world! In addition to this, should you want to perform these pieces, some background reading will help you to do so.

PERMISSIONS

The poems in this book are subject to the same publication restrictions as previously expressed. However, when it comes to PERFORMANCE, you are hereby granted permission to perform these pieces anywhere and at any time. Indeed, everything written in this book has been geared towards you performing these pieces. I hope you do. The only request I have of you is that you attribute the piece to 'Purple Robert' and point folks to www.PurpleRobert.com Thanks!

Prologue

I cannot cook. Whenever I try to cook for two, I cook enough for a platoon, and the Kitchen looks like Hiroshima after the bomb dropped. When my wife is around, I am not allowed in the kitchen. When she isn't around though, I call in Mrs. Sharwood and 'orft' we jolly well go.

For sure, some of these poems are new but many have been written over the last twenty years or so. For those who have heard them before, well, I hope you still like to read them.

This is the first of a set of seven Volumes of poetry each containing sixty-six poems. therefore, I suppose that this is a seminal volume where my obvious future appointment as poet laureate shall be clearly seen. Even so, though William Topaz McGonagal is one of my heroes of persistent poetry, I do hope my gifts and observations exceed even his most obvious gifted genius in the spoken word, and still prove to be a provocative blessing to you.

Purple Robert June 2019, Scotland

The Old 100th

All people that on earth do dwell,
Sing to the Lord with cheerful voice.
Him serve with fear, His praise forth tell;
Come ye before Him and rejoice.

The Lord, ye know, is God indeed;
Without our aid He did us make;
We are His folk, He doth us feed,
And for His sheep He doth us take.

O enter then His gates with praise;
Approach with joy His courts unto;
Praise, laud, and bless His name always,
For it is seemly so to do.

For why? the Lord our God is good;
His mercy is for ever sure;
His truth at all times firmly stood,
And shall from age to age endure.

To Father, Son and Holy Ghost,
The God whom Heaven and earth adore,
From men and from the angel host
Be praise and glory evermore.

From 'Fourscore and Seven Psalms of David'
(Geneva, Switzerland: 1561); attributed to William Kethe

ME & MY 'SCREW-TOP' LOVER

MRS. SHARWOOD

A SEVENTH & FINAL WARNING FOR THE FAINTHEARTED!

THERE'S NO GOING BACK NOW!

YOU HAVE BEEN WARNED!

| 01-66 | VOL 01 | MRS. SHARWOOD IS MY CONCUBINE

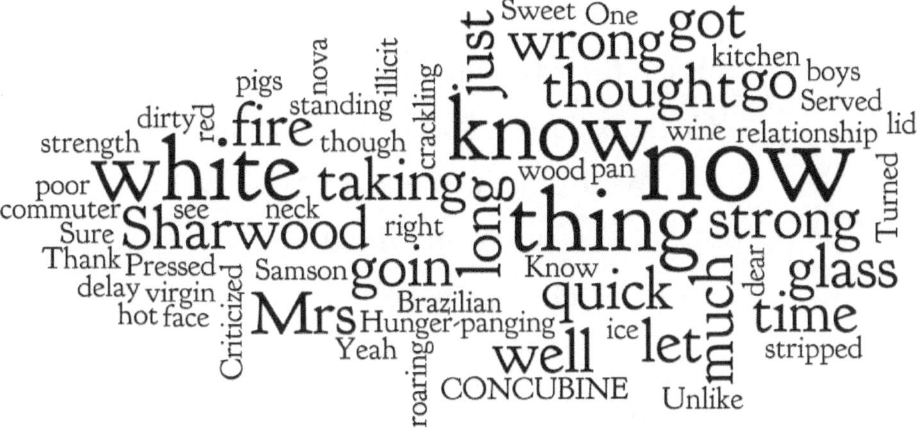

The [i]Dartford tunnel
Was taking its toll on our relationship and
My wife was stuck in standing traffic
Frustrated, fried and crazy
So, taking advantage of the delay
Me and my new lady
Took the time to 'get it on' once more, and
In the lavender filled washing liquid flavored air
Which oozed out of the white, wet tray above
The virgin white cube's, glass porthole,
To the background Brazilian Bossa nova rhythm of
The dirty dish washer
I quickly put her on the cooker top and

Screwed her lid right off!
Know what I mean boys?

Sure, my wife's revolving bra's and pants
In shocked surprise
Pressed their face against the glass and
[ii]Criticized my efforts, but this was a
Well-practiced event now,
A quick and illicit
Hunger-panging
[iii]Guilt-ridden
[iv]Aluminium pan banging affair
'Cause you see, me and Mrs.. Sharwood, well,
[v]We got a thing goin' on and
Though we both know that it's wrong
It's just much too strong
To let it go now

Beaten by a 4lb hammer
The [vi]Diamond wood grenade
Unmercifully split the [vii]knotted hazel
Bringing the proud and unyielding log to its knees
Like a Pole axe pounded into a pink pigs head, and
Stripped of its Samson like strength
Its long grained meat now lay crackling in the fire

"Just one more screw"

I thought
“Before she barges through the door” and
The cork,
Sucked out of the brown bottle’s neck
Bounced to exhaustion on the kitchen floor

Sweet and sour chicken and some long grain rice
Thawed the ice of commuter madness, and
Served in front of a red hot roaring fire
With some chilled white wine
Unlike the M25, speedily
Turned winter into summer in
Double quick,
Quick double time

“Thank you my dear”
She said,
“That was lovely” and
“All that effort!”

“Yeah,” I thought
“You poor deluded thing”
Little did she know that me and Mrs. Sharwood, well,
We got a thing goin' on and though we
Both know that it's wrong
It’s just much too strong

To let it go now

-----O-----

PREAMBLE |

"When you go out to war against your enemies, and the Lord your God delivers them into your hand, and you take them captive, and you see among the captives a beautiful woman, and desire her and would take her for your wife, then you shall bring her home to your house, and she shall shave her head and trim her nails. She shall put off the clothes of her captivity, remain in your house, and mourn her father and her mother a full month; after that you may go in to her and be her husband, and she shall be your wife. And it shall be, if you have no delight in her, then you shall set her free, but you certainly shall not sell her for money; you shall not treat her brutally, because you have humbled her. (Deut 21:10-14 NKJV)

The Pharisees also came to Him, testing Him, and saying to Him, "Is it lawful for a man to divorce his wife for just any reason?" And He answered and said to them, "Have you not read that He who made them at the beginning 'made them male and female,' and said, 'For this reason a man shall leave his father and mother and be joined to his wife, and the two shall become one flesh'? So then, they are no longer two but one flesh. Therefore what God has joined together, let not man separate." They said to Him, "Why then did Moses command to give a certificate of divorce, and to put her away?" He said to them, "Moses, because of the hardness of your hearts, permitted you to divorce your wives, but from the beginning it was not so. And I say to you, whoever divorces his wife, except for sexual immorality, and marries another, commits adultery; and whoever marries her who is divorced commits adultery." His disciples said to Him, "If such is the case of the man with his wife, it is better not to marry." Matt 19:3-10 NKJV

EXPLANATION |

1889 (yes really!) saw the establishment of a British food company called Sharwood's Premier Foods. Another British owned food company, now runs this delectable line of Asian cooking sauces and for a man that cannot cook, well, Mrs. Sharwood is a saucy lady every man can have a long lasting relationship with for under £2.00 a go.

I hate the term 'house husband' for it stinks of un-Biblical role reversal and emasculation. Even so, my wife, my help-meet and true life partner has been 'the breadwinner' for a wee while and trundled to and fro along that biggest car park in the world (London's M25) and you know, she deserves to be pampered and taken care of when she gets in from working out of the house. It is my delight to take care of her, and just for good measure, one day, she reminded me that that's the way it should be! However, sometimes a mere man, a man up to his neck in words, needs help, needs another women to come and help take care of his needs.

In this, the Bible is immensely practical. Nowadays however, Christianity has, somewhat, restored God's original idea of marriage to its intended essence and character, so much so, that concubinage is most certainly counted with the sexual and heart sins of fornication and adultery. Me and Mrs. Sharwood function on an Old Testament footing however!

Lastly, I hope this poem gives you a giggle. After all, things aren't always as they seem, are they!

PERFORMANCE TIPS |

The whole point of the piece is to actually reinforce the immanence of the Almighty in the incarnation of Jesus, Immanuel, God in the flesh. So like us, and yet so different. So like us, and yet we miss Him. We must not lose sight of the humanity of Jesus and this piece attempts to portray that humanity. Bear that in mind and you should be on track. The emphasis should be on the words 'flesh' and 'body.'

i Travelling anti-clockwise and North on the M25 will bring you to the Dartford Toll Tunnel which runs under the river Thames for nearly 1.5km.

ii My lovely wife, bless her, can't help herself giving me advice in the kitchen! I think it's because she has to clean up after me.

[iii] I hate the fact that at this point in our lives, it's mostly my wife that is seen to have a 'proper job', you know, one that brings in a steady wage. I hate the fact that she comes home so tired. I just hate it. Mind you, I have done it myself as well!

[iv] If you are from the USA please feel free to insert Aluminum!

[v] "Me and Mrs. Jones" is a soul song written by Kenny Gamble and Leon Huff, describing an extramarital affair between a man and his lover, Mrs. Jones.

CHORUS | Me and Mrs. Jones
We got a thing goin' on
We both know that it's wrong
But it's much too strong
To let it go now

We meet every day at the same cafe
Six-thirty and no one knows she'll be there
Holding hands, making all kinds of plans
While the juke box plays our favorite songs
CHORUS |

We gotta be extra careful
That do we don't build our hopes up too high
Because she's got her own obligations
And so, and so, do I
CHORUS |

Well, it's time for us to be leaving
It hurts so much, it hurts so much inside
Now she'll go her way and I'll go mine
Tomorrow we'll meet
The same place, the same time
CHORUS |

[vi] This is a fantastic device which splits logs into four! Worth every penny, even if it's just to annoy the neighbours with all the banging. Of course I was making a fire. Yes indeed.

[vii] Marriage is a tied knot and adultery, illicit sex, is like taking a sledge hammer and a diamond wood grenade to a solid log. Just keep banging away you stupid and selfish people and everything falls apart, even heaven tied knots.

| 02-66 | VOL 01 | DIGGER'S TEETH

The whirlwind and the storm sometimes are
My bailiffs and my clearance men
Uncaring as an ugly, busty, northern,
'Lesbiénne-comedienne'
They will beat upon your bending door and
Surround your burning heath and
Fill your mouth with diesel's breath and
Curse you from the top of digger's teeth

They will burst your bending walls and
Invade your un-kept city
They will ravish all your women and
Show your kids no pity
They will rifle all your houses and

Dispose of all your treasure
Their consuming mouth, their hungry hands,
Will seem to have no measure

Then, I shall stand and split your land and
[i]Burn up your leafy oil, and
My all-consuming anger shall turn and
Till your long-dead acid soil, and
All those melted tongues and eyes, and
All that burnt dissolving skin
Shall fertilize my brand new valley
As an answer to your sin

Sure as a sharpened sword
I fall and slash and separate, and
Foam your filthy land with
My [ii]Alkyl benzene Sulfonate

So, remember shaking son,
When you leave the blackness of this alley
That the redeemed shall walk afresh
[iii]My reshaped mountain valley.

-----O-----

PREAMBLE |

Behold, the day of the Lord is coming, And your spoil will be divided in your midst. For I will gather all the nations to battle against Jerusalem; The city shall be taken, The houses rifled, And the women ravished. Half of the city shall go into captivity, But the remnant of the people shall not be cut off from the city. Then the Lord will go forth And fight against those nations, As He fights in the day of battle. And in that day His feet will stand on the Mount of Olives, Which faces Jerusalem on the east. And the Mount of Olives shall be split in two, From east to west, Making a very large valley; Half of the mountain shall move toward the north And half of it toward the south. Then you shall flee through My mountain valley, For the mountain valley shall reach to Azal. Yes, you shall flee As you fled from the earthquake In the days of Uzziah king of Judah. Thus the Lord my God will come, And all the saints with You. (Zechariah 14:1-5 NKJV)

EXPLANATION |

The whole of Zecheriah 14 is an especially fearful portion of the Holy Bible. For today though, it reminds me of God's unstoppable reshaping of the redeemed and of everything else that will benefit the redeemed. This is done at tremendous cost. Quite literally the old goes and in comes the new, no matter what. Some have suggested even through a tactical use of nuclear weapons, or maybe even some other new weapon yet to be released on the global scene. In any event, it's fearful stuff, you know, both God's reshaping of the redeemed and the refreshed place that is quite literally made a 'fit' for them, especially when it involves the judgement of others. You have to get to grips with this and remember that the athletes of God are made fit for purpose and proclamation when they wrestle with Him. This heavenly coach however, shall make sure you carry some injuries! A limp maybe, or even a thorn in the side, previous cowardice, or remembrances of streaking through the night. God's ways are not our ways, and we must get to grips with both Him and them.

PERFORMANCE TIPS |

This has to be the only poem in the world that uses the word 'Alkylbenzene Sulfonate'. I am pretty sure you don't use this everyday so be sure to practice it! Frankly, I don't think this poem is for performance. It's an ugly bunch of flowers for sure.

-----O-----

---

i And in that day His feet will stand on the Mount of Olives, Which faces Jerusalem on the east. And the Mount of Olives shall be split in two, From east to west, Making a very large valley; Half of the mountain shall move toward the north And half of it toward the south. (Zechariah 14:4 NKJV)

ii The encyclopaedia Britannica says that this is "obtained from the petrochemical gas propylene. This molecular group is attached to benzene by a reaction called alkylation, with various catalysts, to form the alkyl benzene. By sulfonation, alkyl benzene sulfonate is produced; marketed in powder and liquid form, it has excellent detergent and cleaning properties and produces high foam."

iii Then you shall flee through My mountain valley, For the mountain valley shall reach to Azal. Yes, you shall flee As you fled from the earthquake In the days of Uzziah king of Judah. Thus the Lord my God will come, And all the saints with You. (Zechariah 14:5 NKJV)

| 03-66 | VOL 01 | THE LAST MUGGING FOR MUGGINS [xi]

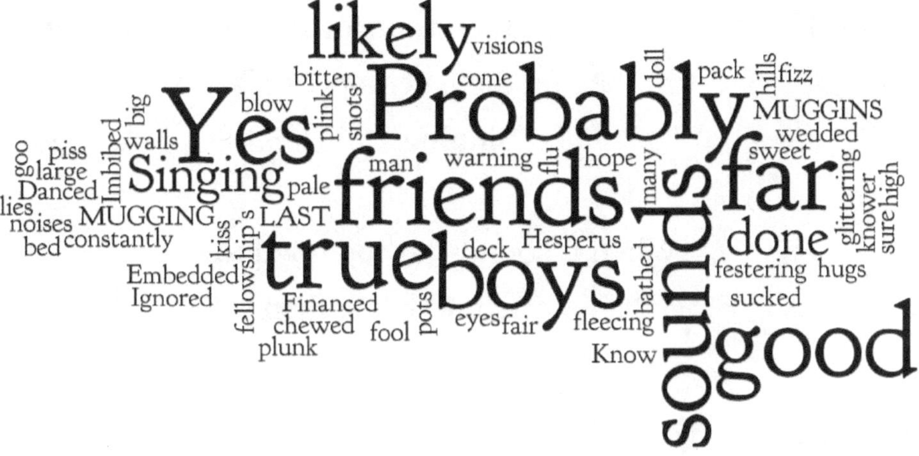

I have bathed in the glittering visions
Of many a bluster-blower and
Ignored all the warning noises
That bounced round the walls of my bullied 'knower'
Yes, I've chewed on the verbalized goo, my friends, and
Gulped down the plunk plink and fizz,
Singing,

"When it sounds far too good to
To be true me' boys, then
It most likely and
Probably is!"

I have wedded the big blow up doll, my friends,
Embedded with 'come to bed' eyes and
Danced on the deck of the [xii]Hesperus
Financed by a large pack of lies
Yes, I've sucked up the green snots of flu, my friends, and
Imbibed on the pale pots of piss
Singing,

"When it sounds far too good to
To be true me' boys, then
It most likely and
Probably is!"

So, no more to the fair or the fleecing
No more to those high hills of hope
For the man that is constantly bitten, my friends,
Is a fool and a festering dope!
Yes, I'm done with the hugs and the muggings and
I'm done with sweet fellowship's kiss
For,

"When it sounds far too good to
To be true me' boys, then
It most likely and
Probably is!
Yes,
When it sounds far

Too good to be true me' boys

Know for sure that it

Probably is!"

-----O-----

PREAMBLE |

Where there is no counsel, the people fall; But in the multitude of counsellors there is safety. (Proverbs 11:14 NKJV)

EXPLANATION |

I have been ripped off several times in my life. The worst kind of 'rip off', the one that feels like a hot wax hair removal, is one that comes from a family member, a fellow Christian who not only believes their own press, but gets you to believe it too! Why do we allow ourselves to be so gullible, so open to such abuse? Well, usually we are in a desperate state ourselves and it seems as though the 'opportunity' presented to us is an answer to our private and pleading prayers, a way out of debt maybe, an opportunity to thrive, to realize our dreams. Do you get the picture?

The answer to combating such muggings is always a very slow walk to the cliff's edge. In business and in spiritual terms this is called 'Due Diligence'. In other words, take as much time as you need to make sure that all that glitters is indeed gold. If it isn't, then give the sellers a kick in the [xiii]goolies and retire graciously.

PERFORMANCE TIPS |

2nd Line, 'bluster-blower' is pronounced as one four syllable word. Line 6 is onomatopoeic and said pedantically. Line 26 needs practice, emphasize the words, and expose your teeth! This is a great mouth exercising line.

-----O-----

[xi] A foolish and gullible person (often used humorously to refer to oneself). "Muggins here has volunteered to drive them home from the pub"

"Who's paying? Well, Muggins of course! "

[xii] 'The Wreck of the Hesperus' – A Narrative Poem by Henry Wadsworth

Such was the wreck of the Hesperus,
    In the midnight and the snow!
Christ save us all from a death like this,
    On the reef of Norman's Woe!

[xiii] Testicles!

| 04-66 | VOL 01 | SPEAK ON SAMARITAN

In you

I see Him.

The echo of His voice

Long lost to me

I hear in thee.

Speak on.

Yes, In your eyes

I see the dancing light

That light of men

Long dimmed in the den

Of my darkness. So then,

My dear Samaritan, shine on, shine on.

Embrace me, will you please,
For in your arms
I might feel the Gathering Healer
That Lover of lepers
The Head Chef of love that peppers
My tasteless soul
That fears not the puss-filled hole.

Oh, your fragrance smells of hope to me
Why else would I be exposed to you?
You smell of deliverance
You are seductive
Enticing, inviting, open, and
Without your knowing
You are become to me,
My word in season fitly spoken.

Yes, you have become my hope of resurrection
Of warm summers coming
Of death boxed and put beneath the clod
Carrier of the long absent but now very present God
Holder of a new life's expect-ay-shee-yon
So dear Samaritan, please, oh please

Speak on
Speak on

-----O-----

PREAMBLE |

Then Jesus answered and said: "A certain man went down from Jerusalem to Jericho, and fell among thieves, who stripped him of his clothing, wounded him, and departed, leaving him half dead. Now by chance a certain priest came down that road. And when he saw him, he passed by on the other side. Likewise a Levite, when he arrived at the place, came and looked, and passed by on the other side. But a certain Samaritan, as he journeyed, came where he was. And when he saw him, he had compassion. So he went to him and bandaged his wounds, pouring on oil and wine; and he set him on his own animal, brought him to an inn, and took care of him. (Luke 10:30-34 NKJV)

EXPLANATION |

The damage of the journey can leave one's soul so callously hard, so cynically cauterized of any real spiritual 'sensientivity' (no, that's not a spelling mistake. Think on) that the footsteps of God walking in Your garden, seemed to have vanished long ago.

I have found that exposure to a fire that leads to impartation of life is the only thing to jump start the dead batteries of such a soul. God has His RAC men, his selfless and saluting servants who are often wheeled out of the garage on cold dead mornings to go and home start such dead hearts. Amazingly, their secret of impartation is that they do not know that they are providing such a service! They are just perky with the expectation of passionate love, and to the hungry soul, they are as welcoming as a Labrador puppy and thrice as nice.So, this piece is dedicated to the unaware Samaritans of the soul who have ministered to me, and if you too are a dead battery in God, I pray will be sent to minister to you as well.

PERFORMANCE TIPS |

I am not sure this is a performance piece. However, it might be a nice bit of verse, to send to someone who has re-started your cold dead battery.

| 05-66 | VOL 01 | THE REAL GOONS AT OUR AUSCHWITZ

It's fine, it's cool, it's awesome
It's fun, its fab, it's friendly
It's young and shiny styling gel
It's national prayer at [i]Wembley

It's brill-i-ant, resil-i-ant
It's project name and vision
It's clueless, bookless internet
A clicking mouse [ii]decision

It's empty, harmless, fluffy
It's flashing lights it's coffee
It's donuts, clubs and T-Shirts

It’s a bowl of chocolate toffees

It’s hands in the pockets up the front, and
It’s a “sorry if I’m preachy”
It’s colored purple corduroy
A plastic fruit
That’s not quite peachy

It’s the white of [iii]Converse trainers
It’s a flat and floppy canvas
It’s smoke, and jokes and a trail of dopes
With no evidence to hang us!

It’s dead, it’s dying, lying
It’s self-deception and it’s passing
It’s de-trained men at Auschwitz
All lined up for the gassing!

-----O-----

PREAMBLE |

And He spoke a parable to them: "Can the blind lead the blind? Will they not both fall into the ditch? (Luke 6:39 NKJV)

EXPLANATION |

I am so bored of church. I am so bored in church. I am so bored.

I have been to hundreds of churches, all homogenized, all cloned zombies, all the walking dead, mostly populated by grandmothers, children, asylum seekers, strange men with strange jumpers and a few cool twiggy armed boys with [iv]plooks and guitars. This happened because of the strange symbiotic atmosphere of the hipster talker and the unchallenged dwindlers, now all kidding themselves with the language of the 'celebration worship experience,' and stirred up revivals. Nonsense. That's what we were left with when we left the straight talk preach for the inclusive language of compromised coolness and then dressed it all up in countdown technology. That 1 hour of dumbness peppered with a little talk then spread like cancer through our spirit being. Even if you break the bloody glass, you won't hold up the weather. Damp darkness is upon us.

PERFORMANCE TIPS |

To be performed to the same Skirl of Louis MacNeice's poem; [v]'Bagpi pe music.' In the same manner, it is also a kind of nonsense poem, but the content of the poem is dealing with the decline of the church and its spiritual decimation by modern silliness and slickness, and not the cultural decline of the highlands and Islands of Scotland during the 1930's and the clash between the dying folk culture and the new slick urban culture "which" has MacNeice said, "is bound to supersede it." Gays, women and effeminate men shall supersede this rubbish. Seen as a poem, the legacy church us full of 'bad feminine rhymes.'

https://youtu.be/n72XebBaMeI?

---

i Several years ago, my brother in Christ, Jonathan Oloyede, a convert from Islam, had several vivid visions of renewal, revival and transformation coming to the UK. These included graphic pictures of Wembley Stadium filled to capacity with worshipping and praying Christians. They tried to fill the National Stadium to capacity in 2012. (No criticism here at all.)

Read more at http://www.wembleystadium.com/Events/2012/National-Day-Of-Prayer/National-Day-Of-Prayer#0I3ccdhRXX4TXcgB.99

ii See, I have prayed the prayer' at http://lookin.com/a-simple-prayer...and before you have a go at me, I helped design this and am very proud of it!

iii Canvas sport's shoes sporting a solitary star. Inspired by the centerpiece of the Chuck Taylor ankle patch, they simply became known as 'One Star'. Reissued in the early 90's, these sneakers earned prominence with a new generation in music and skate culture.' Today, on any hip Christian platform, Converse trainers are the perfect footwear to express your cool love for God.

iv Scottish name for a spot or yellow puss filled pimple.

v Bagpipe music (1938) by Louis MacNeice. This is a brilliant piece and I recommend you go to YouTube and hear him reading it.

'It's no go the Herring Board, it's no go the Bible,

All we want is a packet of fags when our hands are idle.'

| 06-66 | VOL 01 | CANNIBALS EAT IN SECRET

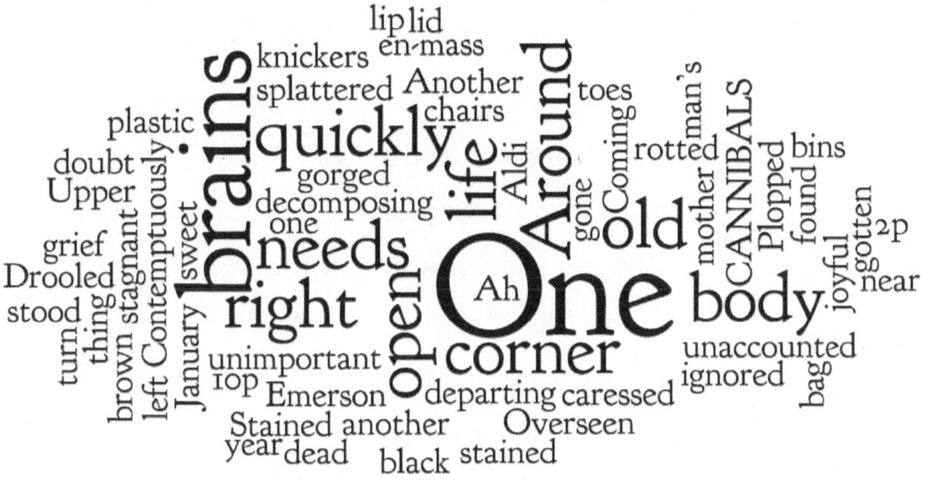

Around the back of the damp stained chairs
Without departing prayers
It was not a body which had been dumped
It was a man's life, all
Contemptuously tipped out of
Damp Cardboard Boxes
Into three green plastic wheelie bins
Which stood open mouthed,
Upper-lip lid flapping on the backside,
Adjacent to the old brown
Stained cream knickers, and the
Soot-black skillet,
One for decomposing body

One for unheard soul and
One for the unaccounted
Spirit.

Picked over for 10p a bone
Plopped into a 2p bag from Aldi
[i]Emerson Fittipaldi
Couldn't race away quick enough
To get the treasures home

The anxious lungs had already gone, but
Were no doubt rotted with the grief of
A quickly passing world
Even so,
I had gotten his stagnant liver of anger
My wife his Kidney of ever-pissing fear, and
Both of us found a piece of his joyful heart,
Just a little,
Spread here and there
Around the toes of Tennyson and
Under the burning bush of Burns,
(Who still rose en-mass and gorged on Haggis, and
Drooled over thighs
Every year at the end of January.)

Ah, but the brains, the unimportant bits of the true
Emotional life

Were all left splattered over the floor
Trod on and ignored.

Who needs brains when you're dead?
Who needs brains when you're bored?

I am told that Cannibals eat in secret, that
They turn their backs on one another,
After all it's the right thing to do when you're
Eating your mother.
So, we too quickly went our own ways.
Glancing a message to the other of
Not to follow,
Not to come near
Not right now.

One book open under a reading light
Being quietly nibbled in the corner
Another upstairs
Opened, sniffed and caressed,
The sounds of sucking the sweet
Out of old paged flesh
Coming from the corner of a room
Overseen by a sewing machine.

-----O-----

PREAMBLE |

And further, my son, be admonished by these. Of making many books there is no end, and much study is wearisome to the flesh. Let us hear the conclusion of the whole matter: Fear God and keep His commandments, for this is man's all. For God will bring every work into judgment, including every secret thing, whether good or evil. (Eccl 12:12-14 NKJV)

EXPLANATION |

My wife and I love going to 2nd hand stores and great scabby old warehouses in particular. One weekend morning we found bins and bins of books, part of a house clearance of a dead Doctor, hence the autopsy feel to this piece.

PERFORMANCE TIPS |

Nonchalantly!

-----O-----

---

[i] Emerson Fittipaldi, born December 12, 1946) is a semi-retired Brazilian automobile racing driver who won both the Formula One World Championship and the Indianapolis 500 twice each and the CART championship once.

| 07-66 | VOL 01 | VA VA VOOM!

God's eldest daughter [i]light and
His youngest girl, the moon
Were dressed in color glorious
That made the angels swoon, my boys
That made the angels swoon

They danced the dark away and
Chased the skulking gloom and
Strummed with breath their crystal chords
That made the sweetest tune, my boys, oh
That made the sweetest tune

They smile and strivings cease and
Make still the [ii]big buffoon and

Softly chide the doubting heart
With hopes of happenings soon, my boys
With talk of [iii]coming soon

Sweet herald maids of grace
Gentle [iv]Mary's of Dunoon
'Twas your smiling hearts of goodness
That filled my soul with [v]va-va-voom, my boys
That filled my soul with va-va-voom

-----O-----

PREAMBLE |

In the light of the king's face is life, (Proverbs 16:15a NKJV)

EXPLANATION |

This wee piece was written in the depths of one of the wettest winters in British history after a week of chesty coughing that was so violent it could have blown the kilts off a regiment of Scots guards. There is nothing more miserable than the middle of winter in middle England, where it produces a dark miserable death to the soul which has already been suffering heavily from light dehydration which has, in turn, caused all your 'get up and go' to do just that! Light and laughter are the chief desires of such a starving man, yes, they become his muse and his passion, for they are the only thing that will get him going my boys, they are the only thing with winter va-va-voom.

PERFORMANCE TIPS |

This is a song. Sing it!

-----O-----

---

i "Light, God's eldest daughter, is a principal beauty in a building." Thomas

Fuller, Cavalier Christian, 1608-1661

ii Panic!

iii Revelation 22:20-21 He who testifies to these things says, "Surely I am coming quickly." Amen. Even so, come, Lord Jesus! The grace of our Lord Jesus Christ be with you all. Amen. NKJV

iv 'Highland Mary' or 'Highland Lassie', or Mary Campbell of Dunoon, one of Robert Burns' lovers, of which he wrote poetry and commented on the same saying : 'This was a composition of mine in very early life, before I was known at all in the world. My Highland lassie was a warm-hearted charming young creature as ever blessed a man with generous love. After a pretty long tract of the most ardent reciprocal attachment we met by appointment, on the second Sunday of May, in a sequestered spot by the Banks of Ayr, where we spent the day in taking farewell, before she should embark for the West Highlands to arrange matters among her friends for our projected change of life. At the close of Autumn following she crossed the sea to meet me at Greenock, where she had scarce landed when she was seized with a malignant fever, which hurried my dear girl to the grave in a few days, before I could even hear of her illness.' In addition to this, try and listen to New Zealand's 'Boy Soprano' Richard Bonsall singing an old Scots Ballad called 'Bonny Mary O Argyle'. Beautiful lyrics amazingly sung.

I have heard the Mavis singing
His love song to the morn'
I have seen the dewdrop clinging
To the rose just newly born

But a sweeter song has cheered me
At the evening's gentle close
And I've seen an eye still brighter
Than the dewdrop on the rose

'Twas thy voice, my gentle Mary
And thine artless winning smile

That made this world an E-eden
Bonnie Mary o-of Argyle

'Though thy voice may lose its sweetness
Thine eye it's brightness too
'Though thy step may lack its fleetness
And thy hair it's sunny hue

Still to me wilt thou be dearer
Than all the world shall own
I have loved thee for thy beauty
But not for that alone

I have watched thy heart, dear Mary
And its goodness was the wile
That has made thee mine for-e-ever
Bonnie Mary o-o-o-o-o-o-of Argyle

v Gil Evans, Jazz Pianist and Composer wrote a great piece called 'VaVaVoom' it's brilliant and would fit really well in all the Austin Power movies set in the swinging sixties. Great fun music. Of course it was Renault with their advertising for the Clio car which in 2011 moved the term to the dark and dangerous side of pornographic!

| 08-66 | VOL 01 | HERE, ON SUNDAY NIGHTS

Listen to noises of the outside strife
All the world goes on with life
While we all play awhile
Here, in this damp old breeze block shell
Every week on Sunday nights

The Permed rinsed old ladies and
The last of the liver spotted and bald old men
Are all hunched over
Well fumbled
Songs of fellowship
Hymns of faith
Mission praise and
The [i]Fisher Folk, who,

Now all
Like the pale green book covers are also
Bald, fat and buggered and
Croaking out the Collect.

Outside in the late but present sunshine
A motorbike,
Two-stroke and revving,
Fumes the corner followed by
A diesel engine bus which
Struggles up the long hill
Coughing out its black lungs
Past the [1]gangsta-graveyard and
All the other rotting corpses while
The swishing cars and
The slip-by train with
The silent plane
Marking the sky, are
All moving on, and
All who ride them
Have gone about the business of their Godless day
Off to [ii]Weatherspoon's for a pint or
A stroll in the lush green park with the big black and
Bouncing dog
All after a Sunday morning fumble

---

[1] Chingford Cemetery, where the Cray Twins lay int eh ground, under trees festooned with many floating black feather boas.. I kid ye not.

Under the cool cotton duvet
With the partner of the day.

Hundreds
Thousands
Millions
Billions
Loving and living exciting lives
While twelve old age pensioners
Surrounded by pale green gloss coated
Cinder blocks are
Dying in this slow cooker crematorium of the soul
Looking like the ghost of Lenin, longing
For present relevance in the Russia of today
Remembering lost power like
Gadhafi in a sewer pipe
Dreaming like Daffy Duck about
Change
Influence
Impact
After forty years of draggin' on
A very poorly rolled
Christian Camberwell Carrot.

Who in earth would
Like

To be
Like
Them?

I don't want to be here.
I would be embarrassed for others to know that
I AM here
That
I even know them!

The dull glossed painted doors
The soft and much flatulently caressed seats
The 1950's velvet curtains
All are moldy green now
Pale in death, looking like
A knackered horse, limping along without its rider.
The silent wooden hymn number holder
Coffin brown
Like the well-chosen carpet
The dinosaur [iii]OHP still in the corner
On its plastic castor wheels
Sentinel like and dust covered
(A backup - Just in case…Even though
Along with the Youth
They lost the acetates a long, long time ago)
The Plastic yellow daisies in the
Mock

Cut
Crystal
The pastor's empty throne
The perpetually unused dark brown communion table and
Matching furniture together with
The ring loop for the deaf,
All sigh in unison over
The utter sense of death
That permeates this old amen hall and
Gathers in the folds of
The swollen stockinged ankles of
Old Doris,
Ninety-three,
Neck down and
Fused at a right angle
Who stopped looking up
A long time ago now and
It seems
Judging by all the high backed chairs in
The setting sun filled empty cry-room

So did they all

-----O-----

And they departed and went up into the mountains, and came to the Valley of Eshcol, and spied it out. They also took some of the fruit of the land in their hands and brought it down to us; and they brought back word to us, saying, 'It is a good land which the Lord our God is giving us.' "Nevertheless you would not go up, but rebelled against the command of the Lord your God; (Deuteronomy 1:24-26 NKJV)

EXPLANATION |

Being Meta-Physical like, :) a lot of my pieces are rooted in, and from the text of the Christian Bible. Also, regarding the state of the current church, I do I get many opportunities to visit the dying. I am talking about the myriad of smaller churches of every denomination which are on the brink of closing their doors forever. Jesus has let them die. No really. I think He has, and purposely so. (But that's another story and another lot of poems!) For many, however, a leap of faith could have saved them. Even so, they refused to live, happy that the last leaves on the tree could fall off the last rotted branch....together. Often, their denomination knows death is coming and refusing to send another minister, is simply waiting for them to be dead, and longing for the trust deed to be read, which dictates that the property and what's left of the fixings will be sold off to the cults, other faiths, a cool property developer, chain of pubs, or a spiv who sells 'stuff' down Walthamstow market and needs somewhere to store his gear, before they will get the money, so desperately needed for their own larger and fantastically failing coffers. Didn't the Southern Baptist International Mission Board just lay off 600-800 missionaries after and overspend of $210 million? I think they did. In light of the current British bill on assisted dying, I have to say that I only believe in Euthanasia for small churches at the end of their life. Where possible, they need the palliative care of a larger congregations. It's all very controversial I know, but at the end of the day it does not matter. Christian Spirituality is becoming increasingly insignificant in Europe. Christian culture and all the shapes of its previous influence are departing and the Christian church in the West is under extensive pressure. I wonder...shall the outcome be coal or diamonds? Fuel for the fire or shiny stones set neat on a wire?

This is an observational piece, part of a verbal tryptic written one Sunday night in one of these churches, after which, I went home, drank wine and ate chocolate, which only dulled the pain a little..

PERFORMANCE TIPS |

This is best performed sat down on a chair, with an air of great melancholy and lots of sighs, epitomizing the last breaths of many of Christianity's dying churches. The object of the observation is of course the last few lines line and especially 'stopped looking up' and 'So did they all.' Make it the point.

[i] Wikipedia says "The Reverend W. Graham Pulkingham (September 14, 1926 - April 16, 1993)[1] was the rector at the Church of the Redeemer in Houston, Texas, U.S.A., from 1963 until 1975. He and his wife Betty began the developments that led to the founding of the Community of Celebration and the worship band The Fisher folk (The Folk Praise Pioneers!) . He wrote several influential books including They Left Their Nets, and spoke worldwide at meetings and conferences"

[ii] British national pub chain, cheap booze and cheap food. I go there regularly.

[iii] O.H.P. Over Head Projector

| 09-66 | VOL 01 | SONGS TO SING AT THE GATES OF HELL

Even Jesus had His songs to sing
In the dark night of His soul
From the breaking of the darkened clouds
That slew the [i]midnight troll
That cast the legions of redemption
Across the spotted bloodied soil
Which danced amongst the twinkling light
That gently stroked the eye-rubbed mole
And for a moment…

Cauterized the flow
Of all those dreadful fear-packed tears
The grief-drops of humanity

That lay strewn across
[ii]Six thousand years
Which though polluted with
The pictures of
The cross which He would die on
Was yet made to smile the quaking mouth
That now sucked on salt and iron
And….

As the joy of those [iii]redeemed
Reflected from the silver disc-ed moon
Across His shoulders fell the purple cloak whose label read
[iv]'Returning soon!' And a
Multitude of peace that
Weighed a massive, trillion tons
Was carried in the
Flashes of His laughter
That split a thousand silver suns
And then…

For a lingering second
Amidst those haunting, howling fears
Or maybe for a month or two
Or a thousand million years

I think I see Him smile.

So,

When the footsteps of your journey

Traverse the sucking edges of [v]Sheol

[vi]Remember,

Even Jesus had His songs to sing

In the dark night of His soul

-----O-----

PREAMBLE |

Therefore we also, since we are surrounded by so great a cloud of witnesses, let us lay aside every weight, and the sin which so easily ensnares us, and let us run with endurance the race that is set before us, looking unto Jesus, the author and finisher of our faith, who for the joy that was set before Him endured the cross, despising the shame, and has sat down at the right hand of the throne of God. (Hebrews 12:1-2 NKJV)

EXPLANATION |

I don't want dress distress up in fine clothing. I don't want to put a shitty monkey in a pinafore and call it nice and cute. No, the problems we go through in this life are profoundly personal and desperately hurtful. Yet, I have observed moments of madness amongst it all. Yes, sometimes, there are such breaks in the midnight clouds that smiles are seen in the darkness, and laughter is heard from the terminal cancer ward, the forgotten prison cell, the box of the wrongly accused, the unmercifully maligned, and even those caught with their hand in the till, or down someone else's knickers. No, I don't want to dress distress up in fine clothing, but sometimes, amidst it all, there is a found relief, an injection of something from another world, another time yet to come, which, though mad to be found in the moments of distressful madness, appear there to strengthen the soul and even the body for the next few necessary steps toward the gallows and grave. . And I am not talking about defiance here, or abandonment to fate, but something solid and profound, even a certain hope which brings a quantum of solace, comfort and the power to keep pressing on, even when we are slowly perambulating past the poisonous parapets of the gates of hell. Such joy, though passing, fleeting, momentary...is strengthening and comforting and courage infusing

It seems that a song in the night, a song of salvation, is something to ask for and expect. Sing out friends, sing out.

PERFORMANCE TIPS |

This piece needs a lot of breath to begin, indeed, the first nine lines should be one literal breathed out flow. The main stopping point, with a major question regarding the seeming perceptive elongation of time is the 'mad smile' of Jesus amidst the agony now and yet to come. That's the key really to this piece, you know, the expectation of the shining of a future happiness, both eternal and infinite, which can make present pressures bearable. This is an invitation for all who suffer to seek some songs to sing and find some strength therein. Ooh and one more thing, 'Flashes of the laughter' needs to be said really quickly!

-----O-----

---

i Wikipedia says: 'A troll is a supernatural being in Norse mythology and Scandinavian folklore. In origin, troll may have been a negative synonym for a jötunn (plural jötnar). In Old Norse sources, beings described as trolls dwell in isolated rocks, mountains, or caves, live together in small family units, and are rarely helpful to human beings. Later, in Scandinavian folklore, trolls became beings in their own right, where they live far from human habitation, are not Christianized, and are considered dangerous to human beings. Depending on the region from which accounts of trolls stem, their appearance varies greatly; trolls may be ugly and slow-witted, or look and behave exactly like human beings, with no particularly grotesque characteristic about them.' I like that. The ultimate midnight troll is satan, the devil himself. " In Him you were also circumcised with the circumcision made without hands, by putting off the body of the sins of the flesh, by the circumcision of Christ, buried with Him in baptism, in which you also were raised with Him through faith in the working of God, who raised Him from the dead. And you, being dead in your trespasses and the uncircumcision of your flesh, He has made alive together with Him, having forgiven you all trespasses, having wiped out the handwriting of requirements that was against us, which was contrary to us. And He has taken it out of the way, having nailed it to the cross. Having disarmed principalities and powers, He made a public spectacle of them, triumphing over them in it.' (Col 2:11-15 NKJV)

ii I like the number six and I am a young earther.

iii 'looking unto Jesus, the author and finisher of our faith, who for the joy that was set before Him endured the cross, despising the shame, and has sat down at the right hand of the throne of God.' (Heb 12:2 NKJV)

iv And he showed me a pure river of water of life, clear as crystal, proceeding from the throne of God and of the Lamb. In the middle of its street, and on either side of the river, was the tree of life, which bore twelve fruits, each tree yielding its fruit every month. The leaves of the tree were for the healing of the nations. And there shall be no more curse, but the throne of God and of the Lamb shall be in it, and His servants shall serve Him. They shall see His face, and His name shall be on their foreheads. There shall be no night there: They need no lamp nor light of the sun, for the Lord God gives them light. And they shall reign forever and ever. Then he said to me, "These words are faithful and true." And the Lord God of the holy prophets sent His angel to show His servants the things which must shortly take place. "Behold, I am coming quickly! Blessed is he who keeps the words of the prophecy of this book." (Revelation 22:1-7 NKJV)

v Sheol — (Heb., "the all-demanding world" = Gr. Hades, "the unknown region"), the invisible world of departed souls. (See HELL.) (from Easton's Bible Dictionary, PC Study Bible formatted electronic database Copyright © 2003, 2006 Biblesoft, Inc. All rights reserved.)

vi Then the multitude rose up together against them; and the magistrates tore off their clothes and commanded them to be beaten with rods. And when they had laid many stripes on them, they threw them into prison, commanding the jailer to keep them securely. Having received such a charge, he put them into the inner prison and fastened their feet in the stocks. But at midnight Paul and Silas were praying and singing hymns to God, and the prisoners were listening to them. Suddenly there was a great earthquake, so that the foundations of the prison were shaken; and immediately all the doors were opened and everyone's chains were loosed. And the keeper of the prison, awaking from sleep and seeing the prison doors open, supposing the prisoners had fled, drew his sword and was about to kill himself. But Paul called with a loud voice, saying, "Do yourself no harm, for we are all here." Then he called for a light, ran in, and fell down trembling before Paul and Silas. And he brought them out and said, "Sirs, what must I do to be saved?" So they said, "Believe on the Lord Jesus Christ, and you will be saved, you and your household." Then they spoke the word of the Lord to him and to all who were in his house. And he took them the same hour of the night and washed their stripes. And immediately he and all his family were baptized. Now when he had brought them into his house, he set food before them; and he rejoiced, having believed in God with all his household. (Acts 16:22-34 NKJV)

A secret stain is spreading upon my [i]alabaster pillar, and
I am haunted by a heart attack
A knife accosting killer

Yes I'm thumping with the hangover of
Lost hedonistic pleasure
For a bitter drop has fallen in my vintage and my treasure

Good fortune knee'd me in the groin
As she walked right out my door, and now
My destitute is absolute
I'm penniless
I'm poor.

For my fleet of ships has sunk
With all my good hands lost, and
Now my bank account is overdrawn
I cannot pay the cost

So, as my cradle of prosperity falls out the fruitful bough
Along my sun burned back God now draws
His sharpened plough

Yes, the coldness of affliction has made
My summer breeze a chiller, and
A secret stain is spreading upon my alabaster pillar.

-----O-----

PREAMBLE |

"Now in my prosperity I said, "I shall never be moved." (Psalms 30:6 NKJV)

EXPLANATION |

Charles Haddon Spurgeon (1834-92) was England's best-known preacher for most of the second half of the nineteenth century. His Daily Devotional called Morning and Evening was first published in 1866. The morning reading for March 10th commenting on this verse says in one paragraph, "If God should always rock us in the cradle of prosperity; if we were always dandled on the knees of fortune; if we had not some stain on the Alabaster pillar; if there were not a few clouds in the sky; if we had not some bitter drops in the wine of this life, we should become intoxicated with pleasure, we should dream "we stand;" and stand we should, but it would be upon a pinnacle; like the man asleep upon the mast, each moment we should be in jeopardy."

White, translucent Alabaster is water soluble and its beauty is therefore easily marred by the slow stain spread of dripping dirt. At the time of my writing this piece, Ireland, Spain, Portugal and especially Greece were all going through their financial troubles. The secret stain of over spending and financial corruption had met market manipulation at the straights of Gibraltar, and the coming together of the pillars of Hercules which once held up the sky, joined lands together, and opened trade routes beyond the confines of the Mediterranean sea, had collapsed. The greater collapse is yet to come.

The truth is we all think the good times are here to stay. They never are. Graveyards are great testimony to that as are cancer wards. We live for today and somehow, are always surprised at the ultimate austerity of all our earthly tomorrows. Be ready and prepare for what is to come..

PERFORMANCE TIPS |

Be cold. Be unshaven. Be smelly. Be bitter. Be animated. Physically move position after, 'and my treasure' and be 'knee'd in the groin.' Remember, there is no hope in this poem, just a straightforward expression of present austerity. Be cold. Be unshaven. Be smelly. Be bitter. Be animated.

-----O-----

i Alabaster is a porous compound of mineral gypsum, or calcium sulfate. Alabaster is softer than marble. Its softness makes it a favorite of artisans for sculptures and objects that filter light and highly polished alabaster resembles glass. It is also water-soluble, so staining happens easily and spreads and the removal of the same becomes a delicate task.

| 11-66 | VOL 01 | DANGLING DEACONS

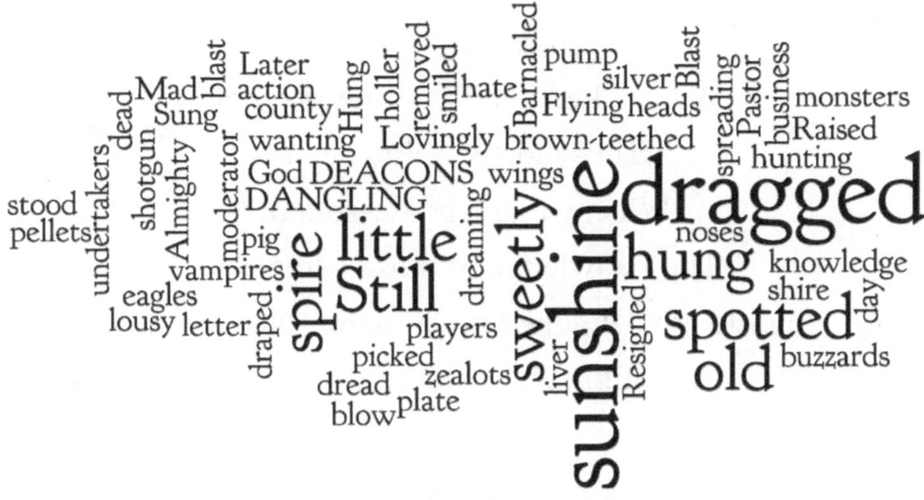

The moderator had now removed

The target he had been wearing from

Herod's totties' daughter of a dread [i]diaconate

Who had petitioned a list full of hate, wanting his

Holy head on a silver plate

For months now

He had stood and sang so sweetly to

The wolves in the waiting and watching choir

Who, undertakers all, old wizened buzzards,

Barnacled, bald and spotted eagles

Lovingly draped their fallen feathered liver spotted [ii]wings

Over their hunting beagles

Still dreaming of screaming down the holler and

Flying through the mire

The rotting remnants of the business of the day
Agenda'd by old Fred
Was picked over by those players,
Those lousy living dead
When we, the possessors of
The knowledge of those vampires
Should have dragged them to the sunshine and
Hung them on the spires

I needed a weapon!
A pump action shotgun with
Wide and spreading pellets
To blast those brown-teethed monsters, those
Mad [iii]Masonic zealots, and
Blow them from the county and
Blast them from the shire
YES!
We should have dragged them to the sunshine
We should hung them on their spire!

But no.

Instead, we all smiled sweetly and
Sung our little heads off
Raised our chins to God Almighty and then

Stuck our noses in the pig trough

Later, I heard that the Pastor wrote his little letter,
Quietly resigned and then retired
For we never dragged them to the sunshine, and
Hung them on their spire.

-----O-----

PREAMBLE |

Then the Lord said to Cain, "Where is Abel your brother?" He said "I do not know. Am I my brother's keeper?" And He said, "What have you done? The voice of your brother's blood cries out to Me from the ground. (Genesis 4:9-10 NKJV)

EXPLANATION |

A few years ago now, I remember being called to a quarterly prayer meeting of churches in a local Southern association. The Host church laid on the grub, great as usual, whilst the Pastor of the church moderated and his diaconate sung in the choir, leading us all in prayer and praise. Leaders all, we all knew, however, that the Moderating Pastor had been going through a most terrible time, his good leadership openly challenged, whilst he and his family were persistently hounded out of the church. Yes, we all knew this deacon possessed church wanted to 'run him off.' What did we do about it? Nothing. Sure, someone offered him a shoulder to cry on, even to pray with him about the situation, but as usual, we watching leaders did nothing about the real problem, which was the brotherhood of the Masonic handshaking diaconate. This particular manifestation of infestation may have been peculiarly Southern in its expression, (we were in backwoods Kentucky) but the symptoms are global. The Kingdom of God, it would appear, has its limitations and its parameters when we, the quiet ones, have become both its limitation and boundary of help. When we do this, God help us, are often the silent enablers of the darkness within.

The attrition rate among Pastors is shocking. This is our business.

PERFORMANCE TIPS |

I do not think this is a performance piece. Except that it should maybe be read at the beginning of many a meeting of those who claim to Shepherd the Shepherds. No, this is a reflective piece, which I hope will get some church members to repent and abandon their cannibalistic clubbing, and love and honor their leaders. Do this, and you will be utterly surprised at how wonderful your church leadership could become.?

---

i For those of you who do not know a diaconate is a board of elected individuals who serve a local church. In the Southern Baptist Convention and elsewhere they usually undertake the job of treasurer, and other operational service roles, including Pastor search and Pastor destroy. You laugh, or maybe grimace, but I could tell you stories to make your teeth curl!

ii I mean demon wings of course. In the deep South, most deacons I knew were hunters.

iii A lot of Southern and country church members I knew were Masons, or if women, were part of the Eastern star. Most saw this is a Christian occupation of community. On a number of occasions I received and interesting handshake and was asked the Masonic enquiry question, “Are you a travelling man?” I would reply that I was looking to the East for the coming of Christ but travelling to heaven on the Kings highway. With that, they knew I knew them, but wanted nothing to do with them.

| 12-66 | VOL 01 | GOD'S 'GOT MONK ON'

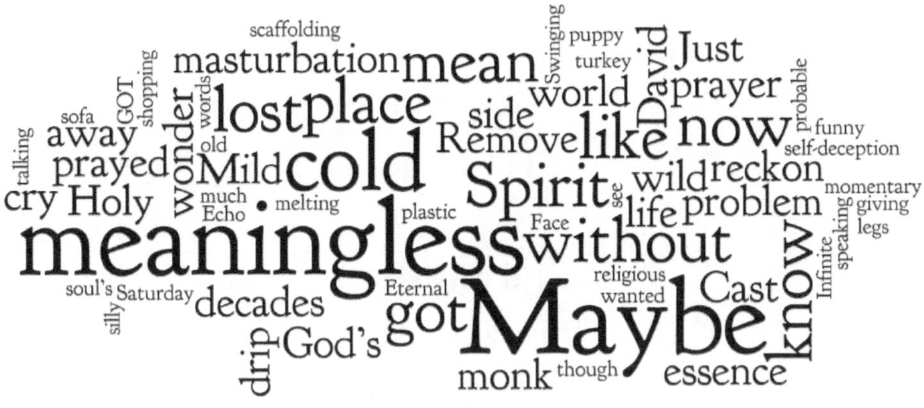

I reckon God's [i]'got monk on'
I know I have.

We're not speaking really, and
I wonder now if He ever has
You Know
Spoken.

To me.

The realization of decades of probable self-deception
Is like waking up in [ii]Sainsbury's
On a Saturday afternoon, and
Finding I've been doing my shopping every week

Naked, and
It's cold outside and
It's me that's [iii]got the last turkey in the shop window
Swinging between me legs.
No wonder people have been giving me
Funny looks
For years.

I'd cry, yes
I'd cry real tears
If I could
Over my 'religious' escapades, I mean c'mon
It's not good mental health
To have spent decades talking to yourself.

Is it?

Where are You?
Where did You go?
When You slipped out my side door I did not see it, I mean,
Should I have prayed with David
[iv]"Remove not Your Holy Spirit from me" and in essence
Plead that you "Cast me not away from
Your Presence"
Should I have done this?

My cavernous disappointment in You

([v]Yes, I am disappointed in You!)
In cold, cold hunger causes
My now dark and empty cave to
Echo with the cold drip, drip,
Dripping disintegration of
My once magnificent stalactite of faith

[vi]I'm melting…..

And the world is a big and lonely place without You
Full of mere momentary meaningless,
Meaningless,
All life is meaningless,
Utterly meaningless
Without You.

Down the side of my soul's sofa
Together with
All the screwed up spearmint papers
A couple of lost coins,
A sharp pin. and
Old digestive biscuit crumbs
I have lost all the important words, like,
Everlasting
Unfailing
Unchanging

Eternal
Almighty, and
Infinite, and
Faithful, and
In their place I have a plastic toy
From a 99p Tesco's Christmas cracker,
A disappointed kinder surprise
[vii]Kinda like
Selfish hedonism and the
Momentary meaningless of a
Mild masturbation problem.

"You could make life wild if you had wanted to!"

Maybe, but
Mild or wild, though
Life without Him is still meaningless masturbation.

You have been
My rock,
My refuge,
My resting place, and
So much so, that
I have failed to stand by myself, you know,
Get on with business
Face the world [viii]'Invictus' like, and
So without You now

I am a lost puppy, just
A Pug-ugly Pug.

Should I have prayed with David
"Remove not Your Holy Spirit from me" and
"Cast me not away from Your presence"
Or is this desire for desperate
New Testament contradiction
The essence of my present problem?
Is the [ix]Dove from above so silly
I mean,
With me,
After all
[x]He surely knew what He was getting Himself into?

I didn't.

Maybe the answer to this happiness-castration
Is a [xi]simple prayer for the restoration of the joy of
Your so great salvation?
An emergency erection of the scaffolding of
Your most generous Spirit
Surely, this could not simply be the essence
Of my the shifty-eyed culprit
Of all my fallen certainties?
Just the absence of a few lines of pleading prayer?

Maybe I should try this again,
Bleeding, pleading prayer, and
Maybe then
[xii]I will also teach transgressors
Just what to do, and
Maybe then
Sinners shall be once again
Converted to You

Maybe.

Meanwhile, I reckon God's 'got monk on'

I know I have.

-----O-----

PREAMBLE |

Let your conduct be without covetousness; be content with such things as you have. For He Himself has said, "I will never leave you nor forsake you." So we may boldly say: "The Lord is my helper; I will not fear. What can man do to me? (Hebrews 13:5-6 NKJV)

EXPLANATION |

Pastorally, I have observed that Christian spiritual depression and oppression is massively on the increase. There are so many 'sons of His love' being upheld not by His presence, but packets of anti-depressants. I am NOT AT ALL judging here. I am just making an observation and it is of the seeming insufficiency of the Holy Spirit alone to bring us peace and joy.

The problem with the journeying Christian is the seeming sudden absence of the felt presence of the Father. My goodness me, this absence has fuelled a thousand 747's carrying desperate children to the ends of the earth to get a piece of that action. They think that God seems to move around a bit, rather than be ever present omnipresent.

In any event, all honest disciples go through this dreadful and unmarried desert place, yet, when you have neither murdered another man's wife nor got his now widow 'up the duff', the reason for this felt barrenness is most perplexing and just to make things worse, we find that the devil is always in the dessert.

PERFORMANCE TIPS |

Melancholy mixed with a cherry of hope. Serve it like that and you've mixed it well. I am not sure this is a general performance piece, however, it could be used really well to introduce some real practical teaching in this pastorally neglected issue.

[i] 'Got monk on' is a peculiarly North of England phrase. The phrase probably means that someone is moody, ignoring you, and has taken monastic vow of silence. As they say in Derbyshire, "She's got bloody monk on ageean"

[ii] Sainsbury's are large supermarket grocery stores in Britain

[iii] Oh, use your imagination!

[iv] This was certainly David's heartfelt prayer in the Old Testament, where as the old dispensationalist would tell us, "The Holy Spirit came upon people like a cloak, rather than inhabiting a person like a bloke in a bedsit". The trustfulness and truthfulness of that New testament statement compounds the reasonable confusion of the experience of God's felt absence in our lives, for there often appears to be no good reason for this.

[v] Christians do get disappointed in God. Tell Him that! He already knows it, so it won't hurt and you know, that declaration begins a whole new investigative

exploration, maybe His silence and felt absence is often the only way He can finally get our attention.

[vi] I rarely quote the wicked Witch of the West, but the surprising devastation and destruction wreaked upon us by this little girl attack of Divine absence, can destroy the biggest of characters!

"You cursed brat! Look what you've done! I'm melting! melting! Oh, what a world! What a world! Who would have thought a good little girl like you could destroy my beautiful wickedness? Oooooh, look out! I'm going! Oooooh! Ooooooh!"

[vii] Pronounced Kinder – Kindah

[viii] It matters not how strait the gate,

How charged with punishments the scroll.

I am the master of my fate:

I am the captain of my soul

You know, William Ernest Henley and all that Frank Sinatra, Marlborough man rubbish.

[ix] 'Shooting Stars' was a crazy panel quiz comedy show, hosted by Vic Reeves and Bob Mortimar, where "The Dove from Above" was a large and shoddy prop bird made from cardboard and coloured paper, which, while being suspended above the contestants bore six key words for further questions. Guests would be prompted to "coo" down the dove, referred to by Vic as "The gift of the coo" and would often use the word "Gift" for many descriptions including "Using the gift of the air guitar", in which a contestant had to pretend playing guitar to a recording.

Frankly, this is just about as silly as some teaching I have heard in the church regarding the Holy Spirit, where ALMIGHTY GOD the Holy Spirit is presented to us a shy pigeon, which can so easily be shooed away. Sigh.

[x] Of course, when He came and made us His own, when GOD the Holy Spirit came to live within us, it was forever! If me twice nightly canoodling with a probable 'poxed' up prostitute won't make Him leave, then His ever presence is pretty certain.

"Do you not know that your bodies are members of Christ? Shall I then take the members of Christ and make them members of a harlot? Certainly not! Or do you not know that he who is joined to a harlot is one body with her? For "the two," He says, "shall become one flesh." But he who is joined to the Lord is one spirit with Him. Flee sexual immorality. Every sin that a man does is outside the body, but he who commits sexual immorality sins against his own body. Or do you not know that your body is the temple of the Holy Spirit who is in you, whom you have from God, and you are not your own? For you were bought at a price; therefore glorify God in your body* and in your spirit, which are God's. 1 Corinthians 6:15-20 NKJV

[xi] Yes, though as a Christian I cannot go along with the first part of David's prayer, still, as a Christian I can most certainly repeat the latter part.

[xii] "Do not cast me away from Your presence, And do not take Your Holy Spirit from me. Restore to me the joy of Your salvation, And uphold me by Your generous Spirit. Then I will teach transgressors Your ways, And sinners shall be converted to You." Psalms 51:11-13 NKJV

| 13-66 | VOL 01 | TEENAGE DREAMS & NIGHTMARES

When I leave home I SHALL HAVE:

A four poster bed
And my own black cat
A word never said
And my own rubber hat
A scooter with a hooter
And a big red nose
A global ban on cabbage
And a new set of clothes
A large wad of notes
And me own spending money
A white sandwich toaster

And a pot of runny honey
A self-cleaning kitchen
With a pink swing bin
A bottle labeled 'Perrier'
That's really full of Gin
A pocket full of petals
And music on the breeze
A garden without nettles
And a teeny tiny sneeze
An ear that always listens
And a nice clean shoulder
A pair of big strong arms
To hold me when I'm older
When I'm older,
When I'm older
When I'm older still

I shall have a nurse
With a large green pill
A large brown box
Sealed with all my mirth
A six foot hole
Full of stale wet earth
Oh when I leave,
When I leave,
I shall posses
A briefcase full of nothing

And a bag of
Emptinessssssssssssss

-----O-----

PREAMBLE |

Now godliness with contentment is great gain. For we brought nothing into this world, and it is certain we can carry nothing out. NKJV. (1 Tim 6:6,7 NKJV)

EXPLANATION |

My wife and myself used run a young people's group that met on Sunday evenings. Our own kids are grown up now, but with some amusement we remember them and all the kids of our youth group and God help us, even ourselves as teenagers and our completely unrealistic and dreamy desires! Most teenagers have no idea that they have to work for a living and that work is hard and stuff is expensive. Unless you are waiting for your rich parents to peg it and leave you the family jewels, then life shall be hard and expectations soon dashed or readjusted to dashing point. I think I need a drink.

PERFORMANCE TIPS |

This is a poem of life contrasting expectant teenage years to the realism of the eventual grave. The tone is taken directly from the journal of King Solomon himself, Ecclesiastes. Therefore begin the piece happy and grinning, and finish it sad and astounded, bitter and disappointed with all your work. It's very much like real life, so as you get older you should read it better. Where's that drink again?

As to speed, this is a 2/4 time poem. It takes a lot of breath and the wording of short 6 and 5 syllable staccato lines are going to leave you breathless, so, do breathe deeply before you star. Indeed, just after the first line which draws you nicely to the edge of the steep run down take a very deep breath.

At the line 'When I'm older', you must completely change the speed. Slow it down like a speeding wagon, suddenly turning into a very muddy lane.

At the last, the final consonant of 'Sssss' needs to be said with the sound of a balloon having its final breath in the world before it exhausts itself into limp sagginess..

| 14-66 | VOL 01 | WHAT A PAIR!

“[i]I once had a magnificent pair!”

Old [ii]Sam Fox was heard saying the same to
Some young woman in a bar in [iii]Magaluf

Ears
Mine were once, golden
Beholden
To neither battery nor apparatus nor a hood nor a blanket
But could easily listen out into the deep, dark, cold Atlantic,
Or, [iv]wherever, and
Identify the squeezed out bubbles of compressed cavitation
Sneakily wiggling their way to the surface

"2 shafts, 6 blades- one two zero rpm, red, zero zero seven, far..
Identify – [v]'Papa'"

But in a bar,
The one in Magaluf, maybe,
No one heard the outrage
No one thought of [vi]'Fahtha'

Ears

"Turn your bloody watch off please!"
[vii]She, kept saying to me

Upon investigation
There was no bargain, there was no plea, just a
"Catastrophic upper frequency range cut off"
Said he

Skipping consonants
The long 'S's of hissing
Are now missing from my world
And I am become the old fart
Nodding at things I thought I heard

Was she being Nasty?
As I walked out [viii]Greggs

Carrying a slice of Pizza
Instead of a Cornish Pastie

Ears

You can whisper in them still,
You know, once you get passed the hairs,
But most can't hear the tender invite anymore.

Ears

Tickled, yes indeed, mine can still be tickled
Pleased
Now especially, after they have they grown
In old age compensation
Like some salacious saliva dripping Ferengi's
[ix]Gaggin' for it
Like a ferret
Dying for it

Ears
The last of the [x]sensual receivers to flicker out in
The cold wind of death
Listen.....Do you hear?
Listen.....The clock ticking
Listen.....[xi]The Time passing

Time Passing

Ferrets are born deaf
But then
Aren't we all

Once in [xii]Targé, in a discount isle
I found a bottle of ear wash for ferrets
Honest to God,
There it was amongst the cut price M&M's,
The purple thongs,
Some sun screens for cars and a big old bra
With 'SF' embroidered in the cups of plenty

Ear wash for Ferrets?
Born deaf, remaining deaf and all the time
Gagging for it, dying for it
In a bar in Magaluf

Ears
Itching for it

A Psoriasis of the
Archdiocese
Where Peter, without the power now, and
Without sight in this dark night
Is still trying to stitch back on all the ears of [xiii]Malchus

The muscular leader of the [xiv]Peace Core Mob
Intent on another crucifixion
Who
Along with his eyeglasses,
Just won't wear the healing anymore,

Happy to live with just holes in his head

Ears
Nicked
By a quick morning blade

Ears
Picked
By a teenage tirade

Ears
Bust and blasted by
A foul word grenade

Ears
Corked

Ears
Stopped

Ears

Popped

By pressure changes

Ears

The double masquerade of attention

Which smiles without heading the word

For whom is reserved

The perpetual noise of gnashing teeth

For in [xv]Gehenna,

All the ears are [xvi]full of fleas

The eggs of which are laid across a lifetime

Of not listening

Ears,

I once had a magnificent pair!

-----*O*-----

PREAMBLE |

Then he brought Aaron's sons. And Moses put some of the blood on the tips of their right ears, on the thumbs of their right hands, and on the big toes of their right feet. And Moses sprinkled the blood all around on the altar. (Leviticus 8:24:24 NKJV)

EXPLANATION |

Actually this is a somewhat personal piece. It was a Friday in 2015 at the ENT department on Stafford, where after hearing tests the graphs showed quite clearly an 'off the cliff' fall in my now inability to hear high frequency ranges. Hearing aids were ordered on the spot, and I told my wife I would not be wearing them but would be selling them on eBay. She tried to remonstrate at my vanity and stupidity. Fortunately, I couldn't hear her.

The Doctor said in the absence of the loud noise trauma, that I simply had a pre-disposition to deafness. In both ears.

In another life, I was a sonar operator on board a Polaris boat. My hearing was tip top and top notch. I could hear a Dolphin fart 10 miles away. Now it's gone. The Dolphin, its fart and my hearing.

I think Western society is suffering from the same catastrophic hearing loss. We can no longer hear the Sheriff of God (our conscience) or the Word of God. It seems we would not listen for years and now we can't.

Lately, in a bar, the daughter of devout Christians was filmed performing sex acts on many men. The distraught parents in their forgiveness of their daughter, rightly acknowledge that darkness is out in the open now and has no shame and increasingly no restriction. Dinah never did do well to leave her family. (Genesis 34:1,2).

PERFORMANCE TIPS |

Be loud and brash about the opening statement: "I once had a magnificent pair!" Get everyone's attention.

i A lady poet once told me that there was no better way to start a poem to get people's attention.

ii Samantha Fox. Singer, Actress, Glamour Model, Sun page 3 girl from 16-20. The most popular pinup of her era. In 1986, her debut single "Touch Me (I Want Your Body)" hit Number 1 in 17 countries. In 1994, it was reported that Fox had become a born again Christian and that same year that year she played at the Christian arts festival Greenbelt. Rumors regarding Fox's sexual orientation began in 1999 when she judged a lesbian beauty pageant, and rumors circulated that, Cris Bonacci, the Australian former guitarist for the rock band Girlschool was her lover. In February 2003, Fox stated, "I have slept with other women but

I've not been in love before Myra Stratton. People say I'm gay....I don't know what I am. All I know is that I'm in love with Myra [Stratton, my manager]. I love her completely and want to spend the rest of my life with her." In June 2011, she appeared as part of a campaign for LGBT charity The Albert Kennedy Trust and at one point; she donated her favorite bra to a charity auction, which allowed fans to buy a piece. It is rumored that Target (Targé) on America tried to sell knock off version of this bra. Though frankly, I know that is just a rumor.

iii http://www.mirror.co.uk/news/uk-news/magaluf-sex-video-parents-girl-3813194

iv In Polaris boats, as a mere rating, we were never told where we were going, not where we had been. "Run silent, run deep (ish) and run ignorant."

v Soviet submarine K-162 was the world's fastest submarine – and it is said that it remains faster than many others since its decommissioning. This sub was designed as nuclear-powered attack submarine and the first to be constructed with a titanium hull. The Soviet named it Project 661, but the boat is best known in the West by its NATO reporting name, 'Papa' class. Actually, I do not remember how many blades the propellers had.

vi In my part of the country, 'Father' is pronounced with very short vowels. 'Fatha!'

vii In this instance it was my wife, though she never used a low level expletive. Honest!

viii I like Greggs. It is the best fast food patisserie in the UK. However, their on-line Log was hijacked and replaced on-line with one that said "Greggs: Providing Shit to Scum for over 70 years" Funny…..but I like it!

ix Apparently, female Ferrets have a unique reproductive system which includes induced ovulation. This means they stay in heat, or estrus, until the physical act of mating is performed. If female ferrets, don't mate, then they will secrete high levels of oestrogen and if this hormone stays in the blood for a prolonged period of time, it will cause a progressive depression of bone marrow that results in a severe, life threatening 'aplastic anemia,' which is fatal.

'Gaggin' for it.' This nasty little descriptor is best heard out of a Mancunians Monday morning gob over a coffee and a fag. Translates: "My female escort of last night, that lovely lady, really wanted to engage in sexual intimacy."

x How they find this out I do not know. But apparently, this is the last sense to go when you are in the process of dying.

xi Oh come on. Who does not like 'Under Milk Wood?'

xii Often used in some mockery and admiration for the fact that this US 'cheaper' store instead of "Target," actually has some style contained therein! Actually, I think I found the Ear-Wash in 'Big Lots?' Yes, that's right. However, for this poem, I am sticking with Target!

xiii Then Simon Peter, having a sword, drew it and struck the high priest's servant, and cut off his right ear. The servant's name was Malchus. So Jesus said to Peter, "Put your sword into the sheath. Shall I not drink the cup which My Father has given Me?" John 18:10-11NKJV

When those around Him saw what was going to happen, they said to Him, "Lord, shall we strike with the sword?" And one of them struck the servant of the high priest and cut off his right ear. But Jesus answered and said, "Permit even this." And He touched his ear and healed him. Luke 22:49-51 NKJV

xiv There has always been a PC Mob if you know what I mean! Very violent.

xv GEHENNA, is "the English transliteration of the Gk. géenna, which the RSV, AV, and NEB translate as "hell." The idea of Gehenna originated in the OT. The Valley of Hinnom (Wâdi er-Rababeh, S of Jerusalem) was in-famous for the pagan rites, especially child sacrifice, that were offered there (2 Kings 16:3; 23:10), and Jeremiah prophesied that God's judgment would fall there (e.g., Jeremiah 19:6; see HINNOM, VALLEY OF). As the concept of the after-life developed in the intertestamental period, the Valley of Hinnom came to represent the eschatological place of judgment (1 En. 27 :lf.; 54:1-6 ; 90:25-27 ; etc.) or hell itself (2 Esdras 7:36; 2 Bar. 85:13). It is not necessary to see Iranian influence in this development, since the purpose of the Zoroastrian molten fire was purgatorial rather than penal (Yasna 51:9; but cf. one early rabbinic tradition that Gehenna was a purgatory for those whose merits and sins balanced each other [Tosefta Sanhedrin xiii.3]).The NT seems to distinguish Gehenna from Hades: Gehenna is the place of final judgment, and Hades is the intermediate place where the ungodly await their final judgment (cf. Revelation 20:14, where Death and Hades are cast into the lake of fire at the last judgment). As the place of final punishment, Gehenna receives both body and soul (Matthew 10:28 par.

Luke 12:5), whereas Hades receives only the soul (Acts 2:27,31; but see HADES Thus Jesus urged His listeners to avoid Gehenna at all costs (Matthew 5:29; 18:9; Mark 9:43,45,47), for it is the place where "the fire is not quenched" (Mark 9:48). Those who call their brothers "fools" (Matthew 5:22) and the "scribes and Pharisees, hypocrites" (Matthew 23:29,33) are liable to Gehenna (the rabbis similarly consigned various groups to Gehenna, e.g., physicians [Mish. Kiddushin iv.14], those who talk much with women [Mish. Aboth i.5], disciples of Balaam [Aboth v.19], the shameless [Aboth v.20]). Like the rabbis, Jesus used the term "child of hell" (Gk. huiós geénn¢s , Matthew 23:15. The only other NT reference to Gehenna is in James 3:6. Here James warns his readers about the dangers of the tongue, which can cause great destruction if one allows it to be "set on fire by Gehenna," i.e., motivated by the evil powers that are consigned to Gehenna."(from International Standard Bible Encyclopaedia, revised edition, Copyright © 1979 by Wm. B. Eerdmans Publishing Co. All rights reserved.)

xvi To 'send somebody away with a flea in their ear' is to angrily tell someone depart! Imagine, the physical and psychological discomfort caused by a literal flea in the ear. Of course, this would have encapsulated all feelings of severe criticism, rebuke and judgement. Talk about 'getting your horoscope well and truly read!"

| 15-66 | VOL 01 | TUNES OF GLORY

So I said to her
"Does this haircut make me look rugged?"
She says
"You've looked buggered for a long time"
I said
"No, RUGGED! RUGGED!"
She said
"I don't know about RUGGED
But you've run yourself RAGGED
And made yourself haggard and battered
Your soul [i]claggy and matted
With the cares of this world and
The weight of your ideas and plans
That demand

The trickle
Of peace
Never To cease
To flow from your fraught fingernails."

I said
"Yes but what has that got to do with my
German barber
You know, my 'Herr Cutt' "

She says
"It makes your face looked squashed and shorter
A testament to your own
Internal slaughter
But maybe I didn't ought to
tell you that
DIDA, EH?
DIDA, EH?
DIDA?"

-----O-----

PREAMBLE |

My breath is offensive to my wife. (Job 19:17 NKJV)

EXPLANATION |

This piece is named after one of my favorite films of all time, starring Sir Alec Guinness and John Mills. 'Tunes of Glory,' is the brilliant portrayal of a clash of wills and personalities between two men, one a deeply psychologically scarred prisoner of war, the other, driven by ego and his own selfish needs even to the point of cruel bullying. All of which is examined in a peacetime but very military drama.

My favorite scene is when Major Jock Sinclair (Alec Guinness) mourns Lieutenant Colonel Basil Barrow (John Mills) who has committed suicide on the back of Jock's cruelty, coupled with his own prisoner of war experience and culmination of PTSD, both of which have driven him over the edge.

With the death of Barrow, Jock Sinclair realizes he is to blame for his commanding officer's demise and he calls his fellow officers to a meeting, where, he recounts a redeeming and grandiose plan for a funeral for Barrow, even a funeral fit for a field marshal, complete with a regimental procession through the town, in which all the 'Tunes of Glory' will be played by the massed pipers. When his friends point out how out of proportion Jock's plans are, especially as the Colonel committed suicide, Jock declares that it was not suicide but rather a murder and that he himself was the murderer and the other senior officers were his accomplices! Jock finishes the scene by finally losing his mind and in the so doing, finishes off his spirit breaking speech, translating the sound of the drums he hears in his head, into a question about his own regiment and his own personal judgment. S, he imagines "The whole battalion of us at a slow pace, just four kettle drums, beating, rapping, with a "die-did it-die-did it die… …..did it?"

I tell you, the film, that scene, and the speech is magnificent and remarkable.

This poem seems silly and simple, but is about the slow suicide of the spirit in 21st century over working. Indeed, it's about the murder of self!

PERFORMANCE TIPS |

The contrast is of the almost Border Collie excitement of life, all made shallow and silly in the rushing about but going nowhere, with the deep concern of the on looking wife.

Emphasize the voice of the concerned wife, even have fun with the cutting consonants in the words of rugged, ragged, haggard, battered, matted, indeed, if you say them with relish, these words leave the mouth naturally snarling with teeth easily bared.

The last silly pun about the German barber is meant to be infantile and stupid, like the individual who is murdering himself, but it also provides a great spring board, a great backdrop, if you will, for the final question concerning the murdering of self.

Of course, it goes without saying, that the poem's performance preamble needs to be a short but succinct reference to the film of the same name! Otherwise, no one is going to understand it.

---

i tending to form clots; sticky.

| 16-66 | VOL 01 | ROUNDABOUT REDEMPTION

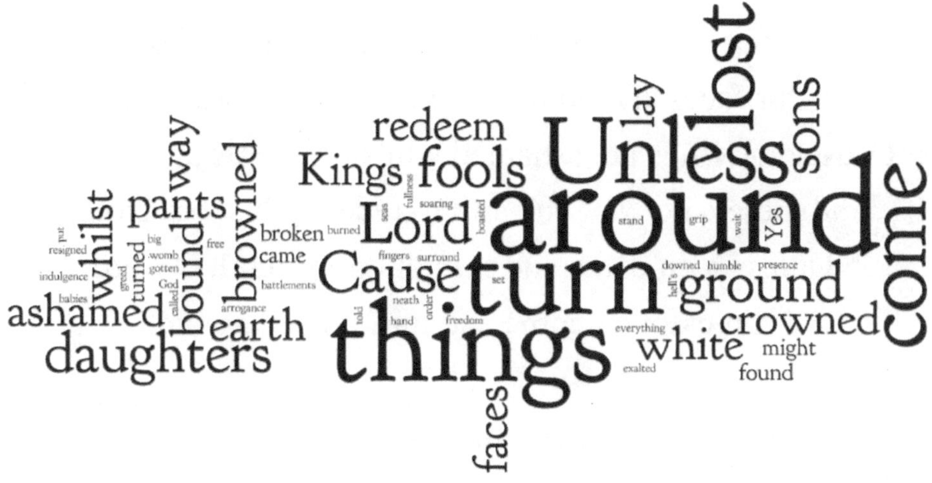

Words that are found in the mouths of fools
Our hearts and our lips have spoken
And now all of our boasted big battlements
They lay waste, they lay burned, they lay broken

For our daughters are lost and our sons are bound
Our faces are white and our pants are browned
'Cause our Kings are ashamed whilst the fools are crowned
And there's no way on earth to redeem this lost ground
Unless You come and turn things around, O Lord
Unless You come and turn things around

We've salted the babies that lay in the womb

We've sucked out their limbs from their mooring
We've labeled the murder with 'freedom of choice'
And sent the kite of our arrogance soaring

For our daughters are lost and our sons are bound
Our faces are white and our pants are browned
'Cause our Kings are ashamed whilst the fools are crowned
And there's no way on earth to redeem this lost ground
Unless You come and turn things around, O Lord
Unless You come and turn things around

We've[i] 'regenderneered,' re-assigned and resigned
We've destructed the family; Your order
We've sailed cross our seas of indulgence and greed
And camped on the sands of hell's border

For our daughters are lost and our sons are bound
Our faces are white and our pants are browned
'Cause our Kings are ashamed whilst the fools are crowned
And there's no way on earth to redeem this lost ground
Unless You come and turn things around, O Lord
Unless You come and turn things around

You have called us to halt, put a bolt on the door
Of our reckless hedonistic abandon
You've told us to humble ourselves 'neath your hand
That we might yet find some safe ground to stand on

For our daughters are lost and our sons are bound
Our faces are white and our pants are browned
'Cause our Kings are ashamed whilst the fools are crowned
And there's no way on earth to redeem this lost ground
Unless You come and turn things around, O Lord
Unless You come and turn things around

Will you answer our prayers with the fullness of Yes!
Not a might, or a wait, or a token
That the devil's mean grip would be loosened at last
Let his thumbs and his fingers be broken

So instead of a penny we've gotten a pound
And our sons are set free and our daughters are found, and
As heirs we're exalted, and the demons are downed
'Cause the presence of God would our camp all surround
If You came and turned things around, O Lord
If You came and turned things around
Yes, we can turn everything around, I say
If we turn all ourselves around

-----O-----

PREAMBLE |

Then the Lord appeared to Solomon by night, and said to him: "I have heard your prayer, and have chosen this place for Myself as a house of sacrifice. When I shut up heaven and there is no rain, or command the locusts to devour the land, or send pestilence among My people, if My people who are called by My name will humble themselves, and pray and seek My face, and turn from their wicked ways, then I will hear from heaven, and will forgive their sin and heal their land. (2 Chronicles 7:12-14 NKJV)

EXPLANATION |

Repentance is yet another word that has been excised from our vocabulary. Sin, judgement, hell, all like a misjudged malignant melanoma on the bare uncovered skin of humanity, have been cut out. Consequently, we have no need of a Saviour, no need of forgiveness, yes, we have no need to worry. There is no god, save the one of our own making and guess what, she's quite nice and most accommodating.

The God of the Bible, however, is a very different case entirely. Once you start messing in His business, He tends to step out of the boardroom of heaven and come and do some restructuring. Lots of layoffs are a coming and His security will not so kindly escort you from His premises. Shape up people or He will ship you out.

Repentance is preceded by a knowledge of our sin and our offence against God which leads to a deep conviction of its wrongness and our inability to replace the wrongness with rightness. Repentance is turning from our sin, back to God.

PERFORMANCE TIPS |

I wonder if this poem is waiting for a tune? The first four lines of the obvious chorus run increasingly fast in the saying and then halt up suddenly for the last two lines

-----O-----

---

[i] I have just invented this word!

| 17-66 | VOL 01 | MEDIOCRITES THE GREAT

I wished I'd reached for the stars
Invested in tension fraught wars
Instead of pensions and
Good intentions

Traded in my mortgage
Got off the mill, and off my arse and
Realized the truth of truths
"All flesh is grass"

But me and Mediocrity made a pact
Just for a while, to wait.

But you see, the problem with mediocrity is

It breeds in them who are overcome by it
It's a viral spiral producing more of the same
Safe and comfortable respect
Hidden in a good name and
Those deceived
Die by it
Slowly
In a denying agony of secret regret

Lost, and long gone is the grasping energy
I last felt on Brighton beach
Windy in the sunlight
Blue in the skylight
A bank holiday, it was, and a beckoning sea
Rapping it's wavy fingers on the pebbly shore
Shouting "Come on, Come on then, Come on to me"

In answer to vast challenge it appeared
On that Monday long ago
From the deep past, even from eternity
An energy rising from within
Bursting out of the tips of my fingers
Pulling off shoes and socks and shirts
Everything that so easily beset me and
Then I ran
Into seas
Killing waves

Cutting them with joyful abandon

I know now it's still the only way to defeat mediocrity!
You know?
Meet it, head on laughing wildly
Holding all things open handed
Allowing the weightier ones
To roll off your fingertips forever
Irretrievable
To the hungry ground and
Foraging acquirers
Who like the fire unsatisfied cry from beneath
"More, more, more!" and
Like the dew in the late morning heat…
Disappear with their new possessions and are
In the end, gone
Planted, naked, never to be clothed upon
"All flesh is grass"

Here I stand, at sixty three
Comfortable with my acquired pot
Of rust and rot
Saying to my son
"Here is all I've got
That and a good name
Respectable.

All earned
Nowt free
Such as I have son,
Give I thee,
Give I thee”

But truly my best is gone, spent on emptiness
I have houses, businesses, futures, a good name,
A Faithful wife, who gave her dreams to me for safe keeping
Well-kept dreams they are too, well kept.
Unopened, for retirement.
Maybe

But when I weigh my treasure on the honest
Internal scales of eternity
They are light,
Empty,
Paper-like,
Ash.

I have invested my time in rust and rot
Never shall it be said of me
“Here is a man who gambled on God and lost the lot!
Naked he came naked he went, but everything was spent
Everything!”
I suspect shoe string people
Dependent and dangerous disciples

I am not suspect
Never have been
Nor dangerous
Never shall it be said of me
"Here was a man profligate with his spirituality
This man invested in the invisible
This man chose the soul, instead of the body
This man attempted to slay giants
Take mountains, claim kingdoms
That were not his own
This man could say silver and gold have I none
But such as I have give I thee

Oh to be that man, now at sixty three
But I shall die in comfort
In a private room
People shall say nice things of me and
The devil will be disappointed at my passing and
God shall pity my widow

I see now friends, right now
Far back
Beyond Brighton beach
Back then when He saved me
How with sadness this time

He then watched my future widow

Put in two mites and

Me put in one

Maybe

-----O-----

PREAMBLE |

Jesus said to him, "If you want to be perfect, go, sell what you have and give to the poor, and you will have treasure in heaven ; and come, follow Me." But when the young man heard that saying, he went away sorrowful, for he had great possessions. Then Jesus said to His disciples, "Assuredly, I say to you that it is hard for a rich man to enter the kingdom of heaven. And again I say to you, it is easier for a camel to go through the eye of a needle than for a rich man to enter the kingdom of God." (Matt 19:21-24 NKJV)

EXPLANATION |

This is the story of a wealthy man's regret at his most successfully wasted life. I do not want to be that mediocre man before the Throne of God.

PERFORMANCE TIPS |

At sixty three, a man with terminal eternity, stares in the mirror, and in the deep pools of sad eyes, sees the dust of dead dreams drift away in the ebb of his life Be that man.

-----O-----

| 18-66 | VOL 01 | A VISION OF FAG & FACE

Her sky blue tracksuit had faded
As had her sky, long ago
Before she had a chance to know it.
It now hung low, as did her horizon,
Well below her buttocks
Like a full and smelly nappy
Old and soiled.
What did she think of herself?
Dare she think of herself?
This vision of fag and face.

The [i]fag
Cork tipped of course,
Hung unused from the

Corner of her hard chapped lips,
Just hung there like her life,
Slowly burning away

Ashes to ashes and dust to dust.

She was coming out of the phone box,
The door ajar, about to be slammed
She'd not got through to anyone
Or no one was listening.
Her life had been like that all along

No one really speaking
No one really listening

She had no money for her own phone.
Oh it wasn't the fact that showed it,
But the face
This vision of fag and face
This female Popeye with greying perm
Crated with all the crap of her life.

This wasn't right
She deserved more,
A little more brains
A few more chances
That she knew to be so

Not just fleeting happenings along her horizon
A bit more confidence and oomph
To be enabled reach out and grab 'em
And reel 'em in,
Maybe a bit more money
And a few good men in her life
Maybe even one good man to help her.

Good God,
I know of one!
He'll not use her
He'll not abuse her
Surely He'll love her
This shadow of a woman
This vision of fag and face
And give her a hope and a future
A promise of a changeling's resurrection
From fag and crumpled face
To saint and holy race.

-----O-----

PREAMBLE |

So I bought her for myself for fifteen shekels of silver, and one and one-half homers of barley (Hos 3:2. NKJV)

EXPLANATION |

I was in a car, and she, in a state, coming out of a disappointed phone box on the edge of a rundown council estate .Yes even Britain has Section 8 housing. Well, we used to have before we gave everyone the right to buy. Now we have a housing crisis on our hands and it worsens every day, overseen by anti-Brexit buffoon governments, populated by paedo's and so called former upper middle class cocaine sniffers. What a miserable bunch of self-serving sycophantic.....Oh, don't get me started!

PERFORMANCE TIPS |

With pathos.

-----*O*-----

---

i 'Fag' is British slang for ' taken from 'fag' a loose piece, or the last remnant of cloth.'

| 19-66 | VOL 01 | A COFFEE SHOP CAMEO

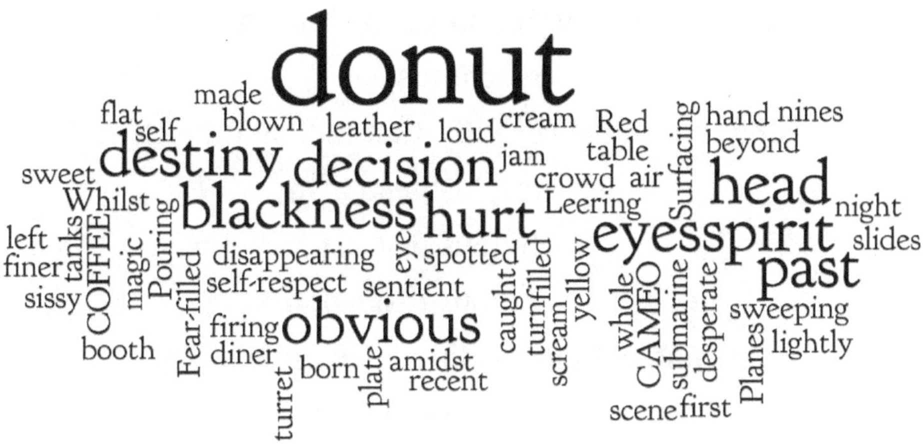

The cream donut lay on the plate
Before his late and staring eyes which
Peered out the diamond spotted window pain, his head
Leering into the retreating red ant eyes
Hand in hand disappearing into the blackness of beyond

Whilst his spirit was dabbling amidst his
Desperate donut dreaming
The turret of his sweeping revenge
Was firing five nines
Into the crowd of those
Who had hurt him and deserted him
The loud lostness of his self-respect
Pouring madness into the whole sad scream

The sentient scene of a decision being born

The reflection of his yellow hair
Was the only highlight on the blackness and
It caught his eye
Causing him to disdainfully first look at himself and
Then turn his head away
In obvious distrust
In obvious disgust
The magic donut pulling back his thoughts
His spirit and his very hurt self from
The oh so sour and recent past into
The not so sweet sugar donut present

He just sighed over
The lightly dusted jam filled stone of destiny and
Then decision made
Arose like a submarine
Surfacing from the desperate
Fear-filled deep with all tanks blown and
Planes on hard to rise
Palms flat on the table
With purpose and decisiveness
He now slides left from his
Red leather booth of destiny and
Strides past me
Sashaying out of the not so finer diner

Into the dank night air

I looked at him and I said,
"Now there's a sissy
With a dream"

-----O-----

PREAMBLE |

...but He did not respect Cain and his offering. And Cain was very angry, and his countenance fell. So the Lord said to Cain, "Why are you angry? And why has your countenance fallen? 7 If you do well, will you not be accepted? And if you do not do well, sin lies at the door. And its desire is for you, but you should rule over it." Now Cain talked with Abel his brother; and it came to pass, when they were in the field, that Cain rose up against Abel his brother and killed him. Then the Lord said to Cain, "Where is Abel your brother?" He said, "I do not know. Am I my brother's keeper?" And He said, "What have you done? The voice of your brother's blood cries out to Me from the ground. So now you are cursed from the earth, which has opened its mouth to receive your brother's blood from your hand. When you till the ground, it shall no longer yield its strength to you. A fugitive and a vagabond you shall be on the earth." (Gen 4:5-12 NKJV)

EXPLANATION |

I believe I picked up this little phrase, "Now there's a sissy with a dream" from the British comedian Ken Dodd. I don't remember the context or the implication but never the less, it remained in my mind. When I saw this Cissy in Hollywood Florida, it was from this phrase that this little coffee shop cameo emerged.

PERFORMANCE TIPS |

In a chair, with a cup of coffee, explaining to your friend what just happened before they came in.

-----O-----

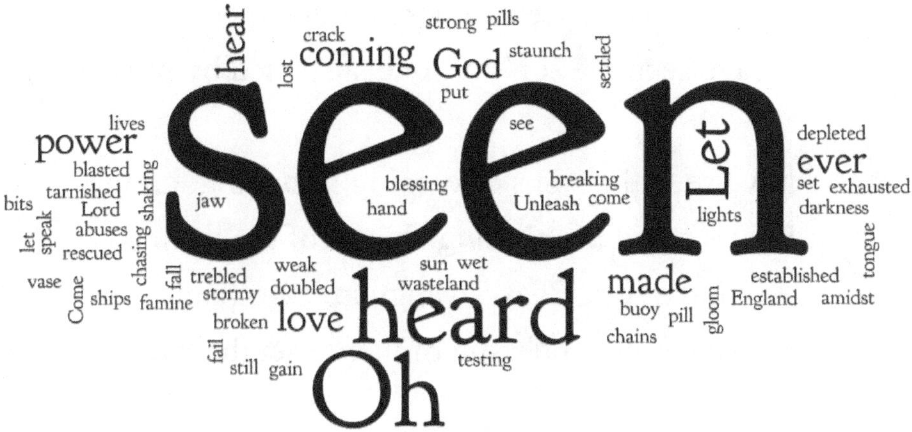

I have seen the swift exhausted, down, defeated
I have seen the staunch and strong made weak
I have seen [i]'Great-Heart's' power depleted
I have heard the running tongue no longer speak.

I have seen those who put God second, well established
I have seen the rich made richer ever still
I have seen those who love religion gain all they wished
I have seen [ii]Naomi gulp the bitter pill

I have seen the lights go out all over England
I have seen the darkness quench the brightest stars
I have seen the bruised jaw, the broken hand
I have seen the wilted heads in tarnished vase

I have heard the wet reply, the mock excuses
I have seen the lost sheep rotting on the hills
I have seen authority's abuses
I have seen the son's of love sustained by pills

I have seen the signs of coming hastening famine
I have heard the chasing chatter of the damned
I have seen Beast's vanguard ever rising
I have seen God's sun of mercy set the land

I have seen hearts fail and crumple in the testing
I have seen the faithful blasted all to bits
And amidst it all, have heard
The whisper of a coming blessing
I have heard "Revival!" clothe a thousand lips.

Oh! Let me see the wasteland wanderers be settled
Oh! Let me hear their ebbing lives resound with joy
Let your good blessings fall, be doubled, trebled!
Unleash apostolic ships from stormy troubled buoy

Oh let me hear the crack of iron chains a breaking
The shouts of happiness
Of those rescued from deep gloom
Oh God!
In your power come now a shaking!

Raise your standard, Oh Lord!

Come, and meet our doom!

-----O-----

PREAMBLE |

When the enemy comes in like a flood, The Spirit of the LORD will lift up a standard against him. "The Redeemer will come to Zion, And to those who turn from transgression in Jacob," Says the LORD. (Isa 59:19-20 NKJV)

I will destroy the winter house along with the summer house; The houses of ivory shall perish, And the great houses shall have an end," Says the LORD. (Amos 3:15 NKJV)

EXPLANATION |

I don't know about you but I am tired of being presented with church heroes, valiant conquerors, with no mark of battle or smell of smoke upon them. There are far too many men of straw in the 21st century.

I am also tired of pastors polishing turds. Things are bad. They are very bad. Let's call it like it is.

I have been a Pastor for many years. I have seen shooting stars. I am not surprised at those who come and go quickly. A greater problem is when those staunch continuers, can continue no longer. Tired of looking, weary in watching, they are weighed down with disappointment. So hungry, many have lost their appetite.

This is what I have really seen in our churches, this is what I have really heard. God help us..

PERFORMANCE TIPS |

From the line "I have heard "Revival!" Clothe a thousand lips" the piece turns into a prayer. Make it yours

-----O-----

iGreat-Heart is Bunyan's great character in part of Pilgrims Progress. The friend of The interpreter it is he who weak himself, takes care of those weaker than he and expends himself again and again, escorting Pilgrims to the edge of the great river of death. He is fearless, selfless, and magnificently undefeated by no one except Christ.

ii Now the two of them went until they came to Bethlehem. And it happened, when they had come to Bethlehem, that all the city was excited because of them; and the women said, "Is this Naomi?" But she said to them, "Do not call me Naomi; call me Mara, for the Almighty has dealt very bitterly with me. Ruth 1:19-20 NKJV

| 21-66 | VOL 01 | BAGS OF BOMBS AND SACKS OF CRAP

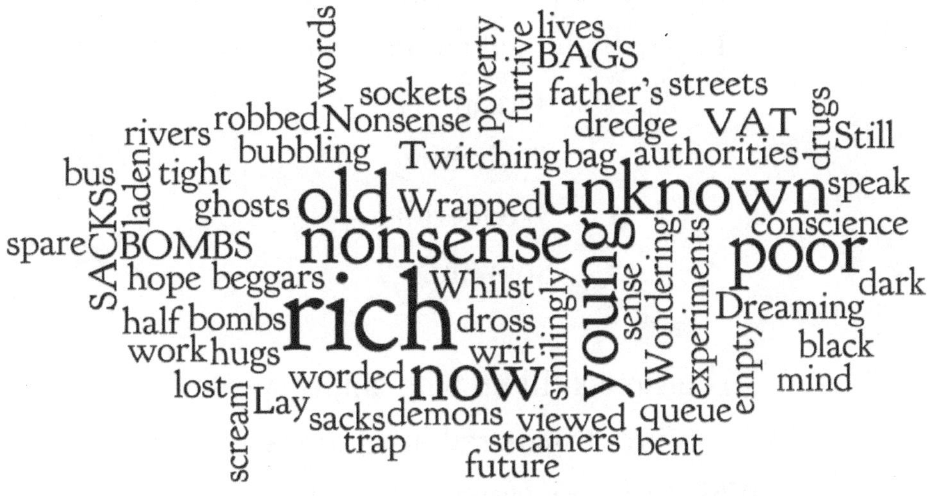

The rich are very rich
The poor are very poor
Yet those who have no hitch
Still scream for more and
More

The dross
Mumble for spare old coppers
The scabs
They smilingly accost you
The travelers pursue the laden shoppers and
The beggars dredge the growing bus queue

Tramp steamers on rich rivers

The ill in mind speak unknown words
To unknown ghosts accompanying and
Lay half clothed amongst the turds
Dreaming,
Twitching,
Wondering,
Something?

The streets fill up with empty wards
From shattered institutions
Whilst smiling servants from billboards
Amend our constitution

What once was writ on Christian hearts
So full of sensibilities
Is now viewed through sockets of the blind and
Paupered, robbed authorities

The working class now have no work
The young, no hope, no future
Possessed by demons of lost, stark, dark
They'd rather rob and shoot you

They have no home, no father's hugs
No sharpened worded conscience and so

Drown in a bubbling VAT of drugs
Their lives a bag of nonsense

Nonsense, no sense,
Utter nonsense
Bags of bombs and sacks of crap
Discarded off-scouring of bent experiments
Wrapped up in the poverty trap
Presents for the old young, and furtive
Tied tight by the shiny black ribbon
Of a rotting, revolting, politicalism.

-----O-----

PREAMBLE |

Then Jesus said to His disciples, "Assuredly, I say to you that it is hard for a rich man to enter the kingdom of heaven. 24 And again I say to you, it is easier for a camel to go through the eye of a needle than for a rich man to enter the kingdom of God." (Matt 19:23-24 NKJV)

EXPLANATION |

This poem originally ended with the word CONSERVITISM. Old Tony however, who once could easily stand for President of the United States AND get elected, did no better and some would say far worse than the Conservatives.

How a nation takes care of its young and it's old, those with roofs and especially without them are testimony to its love, it's care and therefore it's continuance!

This Poem is dedicated to the 1%. I weep for you.

PERFORMANCE TIPS |

[i]Be Citizen Smith. "Power to the people!"

-----O-----

---

[i] Wikipedia rightly says. 'Citizen Smith was a British television sitcom written by John Sullivan which was broadcast from 1977 to 1980.Citizen Smith starred Robert Lindsay as "Wolfie" Smith, a young Marxist[1][2] "urban guerrilla" in Tooting, South London, who is attempting to emulate his hero Che Guevara. Wolfie is a reference to the Irish revolutionary Wolfe Tone who used the pseudonym Citizen Smith in order to evade capture by the British. Wolfie is the self-proclaimed leader of the revolutionary Tooting Popular Front (the TPF, merely a small bunch of his friends), the goals of which are "Power to the People" and "Freedom for Tooting". In reality he is an unemployed slacker and petty criminal whose plans fall through due to apathy, ineptitude and inexperience.'

| 22-66 | VOL 01 | THE DOGS OF DERISION

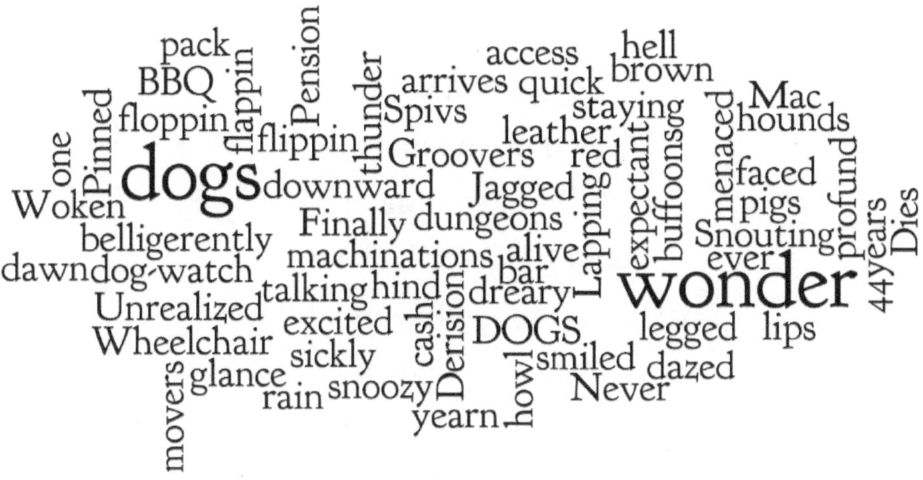

The Dangerous dogs in [i]wet-nosed yards
Bark belligerently at [ii]Spivs
Who with quick talking cash
Compete competitively with
The now excited and expectant pigs
Ears, flappin', flippin', floppin', running
In the grunting green fields
Snouting out the snoozy dreamers
Drenched with sickly snot
Woken from dazed dozings, as if
Finally smiled upon and no longer menaced
By the morbid machinations of
Yellow-spotted red faced
Big Mac movers

Groovers
System users
Wheelchair wizzers
Snack bar snails
Jagged brown tails
Pinned on the one legged
Wonkey donkey
At a BBQ for buffoons
All advocating 44 years of 9 to 5
And the wisdom of
Staying alive, being 'profund'
You know staying around to access their
Pension fund

"Will it rain?"
They wonder
"Will it thunder?
Will we hunger?"
They wonder
"Will we yearn?
Will we really burn?"

The dangerous dogs, glance back
Over their hind quarters
Lapping leather lips
Leading the blind pack ever downward
To dreary dog-watch dungeons

Where the dawn
Never arrives but
Dies,
Continually, in
Unrealized expectancy, and

In the distance
The hounds of hell howl

In Derision

-----O-----

PREAMBLE |

But even if our gospel is veiled, it is veiled to those who are perishing, whose minds the god of this age has blinded, who do not believe, lest the light of the gospel of the glory of Christ, who is the image of God, should shine on them (2 Cor 4:3-4. NKJV)

EXPLANATION |

Whilst we prepare for retirement and a comfortable death, we lemmings are led over the edge of self-protection into hell. Listen, the hounds of hell are howling with laughter whilst we labour to leave our children more of which has so thoroughly blinded us and bound us.

PERFORMANCE TIPS |

A lot of these words are onomatopoeic, so, just enjoy them!

-----O-----

[i] Young girls lie bedded soft or glide in their dreams, with rings and trousseaux,

bridesmaided by glow-worms down the aisles of the organ playing wood. The boys are dreaming wicked or of the bucking ranches of the night and the jollyrogered sea. And the anthracite statues of the horses sleep in the fields, and the cows in the byres, and the dogs in the wet-nosed yards; and the cats nap in the slant corners or lope sly, streaking and needling, on the one cloud of the roofs. (From the first page of Dylan Thomas – Under Milk Wood)

[ii] In Britain, the word spiv is slang for a type of petty criminal who deals in illicit, naughty and typically black market goods. The word was came to the fore during the Second World War and in the post-war period when many goods were rationed due to shortages. I am sure it will be used in the future.

| 23-66 | VOL 01 | SAGGY or COPPER-TOP CANNES

Topless and toothless old women
Breasts like sun dried tomatoes
Pirouette, like aged hippos
On white froth, at the edge of cold coffee waves
Whilst old men wearing nothing but
Old posing pouches
Hairless
Save that which grows from ear and nose
Drool their desire over old meat
Who with curling toes
Walk designer dogs with diamond collars
Some laying in the careful arms of dawdling dames
With dopamine eyes

‘Neath the blue azure skies of
Copper topped [i]Cannes, and

Long ago in Monaco
Armani men pick at escargot
Eyeing fat white yachts with faces like…..

Dead pan pizza for 50f
Bright marbled buildings fed by offshore banks
Palm trees still in a fair March breeze
Jean Paul Gaultier silk chemise
Gaudy graffiti everywhere
Aged loneliness, rich despair
Très chic girls
Traveling far
Pampas grass in Tappas bars
Bag ladies sewing
Amidst the rocks
Shingle beaches
[ii]Sportif cocks
Private sands all full of dross
[iii]General Ferrié and a Maltese cross
Japanese gardens full of Princess Grace
Monte Carlo
Grand Prix race
Double-Decker trains on the cote D’Azure
Pavements full of dog manure

Bathing beauties in brown-eyed beds
Silver BMW'S with no retreads
Lazing, Lying at the gates of hell
Hiding Pavarotti from the tax man's smell
Sell, sell, buy buy, sell,
Rolex on the wrist of a ne'r do well
Dying wrinkled reaching hands
Grasping at the sunshine in
Copper-top Cannes

-----O-----

PREAMBLE |

So teach us to number our days, That we may gain a heart of wisdom. (Ps 90:12 NKJV)

EXPLANATION |

It was March, and some very good friends had made it possible for us to be with them in their place of work in Cannes. They overwhelmed us with their generosity and freed us to roam, and to think, to observe, and to drink. This is what I saw, on the Cote D'Azure, maybe 1998.

PERFORMANCE TIPS |

When you get the line 'Dead Pan Pizza – The Rhythm of the piece really picks up. Stomp it out baby!

-----O-----

i Cannes is a city located on the French Riviera. It is a commune of France located in the Alpes-Maritimes department, and host city of the annual Cannes

Film Festival, Midem, and Cannes Lions International Festival of Creativity. The city is known for its association with the rich and famous, its luxury hotels and restaurants, and for several conferences. On 3 November 2011 it also played host to the G20 organisation of industrialised nations.(Wikipedia)

[ii] It started in 1882 with the opening of a little hosiery store in Romilly-sur-Seine, in a part of the Champagne region called the Aube.

Emile Camuset, the man who opened that store, loved sports with a fierce passion. When he started making sports jersey in his small workshop, he probably never dreamed that, 130 years later, le coq sportif would become one of the world's most prestigious brands, renowned for its clothing, footwear and sporting equipment. – Le Coq Sportif!

[iii] Gustave-Auguste Ferrié (19 November 1868 – 16 February 1932) was a French radio pioneer and army general.

| 24-66 | VOL 01 | DO EWE REMEMBER?

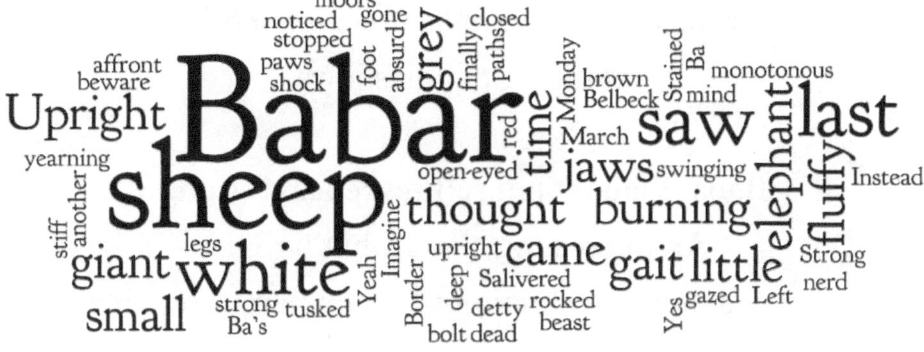

"Yeah, the last time I saw Babar
He was burning!

Finally his foot in mouth disease
Had laid his little legs stiff and
Upright to the pressing grey, and
Today
He is but smoke

No joke
He's gone!

Babar was small and fluffy white
But thought himself a great giant

A hunk with a swinging trunk
That rocked his little body
To and fro like a soon to be shipwrecked sheep
That had spent years upon the deep
Instead of just months upon the moors
Dodging doggies jaws

Babar thought himself tusked and strong
An interesting choice, but wrong
No, not a monotonous hippopotamus he
But an elegant grey elephant
Strong and Jolly
Who then, assuming such for himself
Took no crap from any Border Collie
That gazed at his elephantine gait

Had the affront stopped at
Salivered jaws and muddy paws on his heels
Fair enough
But Babar, went too far-far
In that he would become 'King' of the herd!
How absurd!
The nerd!

It came then, to him, as quite a shock
When depressed and open-eyed
He finally saw that we were but a flock

Of sheep, dirty brown and 'detty'
Not giants of the Serengeti
Of his mind

But there was no helping him then
There was no help for him then
For Babar's gait
Had closed all the paths to the hearts of his brothers and now
Others, more upright than us
Had noticed this small and fluffy elephant
Trumpeting his madness
Trying to convince all and Sundry
On a wet March Monday
That He was king of Dale and Pen and
Did not care for even them
Yes, they'd best beware on Belbeck Down
Or Babar beast would stomp them down
He would be a hero of renown
A sheep, at last, would wear a golden crown!

Upright
Dressed in white
They came and
Placed a bolt in Ba Ba's brain and
Stained the white sheep red and
Left another giant dead

Imagine, if you will
A sheep with yearning

No, No…..
The last time I saw Babar

He was burning"

-----O-----

PREAMBLE |

For I say, through the grace given to me, to everyone who is among you, not to think of himself more highly than he ought to think, but to think soberly, as God has dealt to each one a measure of faith. (Romans 12:3 NKJV)

EXPLANATION |

In a few years' time, sheep, enjoying a pint in the snug of a pub, will muse over the 2001 'Foot and Mouth' epidemic.

Wikipedia says that "The outbreak of foot and mouth disease in the United Kingdom in the spring and summer of 2001 caused a crisis in British agriculture and tourism. The epidemic saw 2,000 cases of the disease in farms in most of the British countryside. Around seven million sheep and cattle were killed in an eventually successful attempt to halt the disease. ....By the time the disease was halted by October 2001, the crisis was estimated to have cost Britain £8bn ($15bn)" The 7 million cattle and sheep were sometimes buried but mostly burnt on great sacrificial pyres!"

Wikipedia also says that "Babar the Elephant is a popular French children's fictional character who first appeared in L'Histoire de Babar by Jean de Brunhoff in 1931 and enjoyed immediate success. English language versions, entitled The Story of Babar, appeared in

1933 in Britain and the United States. The story is based on a tale that Brunhoff's wife, Cecile, had invented for their children. It tells of a young elephant called Babar who leaves the jungle, visits a big city, and returns to bring the benefits of civilization to his fellow elephants."

This poem is about a sheep who believes he is an elephant and acts accordingly. This is a sheep who actually believes he is more and there is more than can be seen. Imagine that!

Those brave Knights that tilt at windmills have never been accepted by the herd and the more they continue in their seeming madness the more they are rejected and summarily dealt with. Be careful if you are going to be different from the herd. Count the cost, for their shall surely be one to pay!

PERFORMANCE TIPS |

This is pretty straightforward. If you want to wear a woolly jumper, chew and sniff a lot whilst you're doing it, then that might be good!

-----*O*-----

| 25-66 | VOL 01 | A SHEEP FINALLY LOOKS HOMEWARD

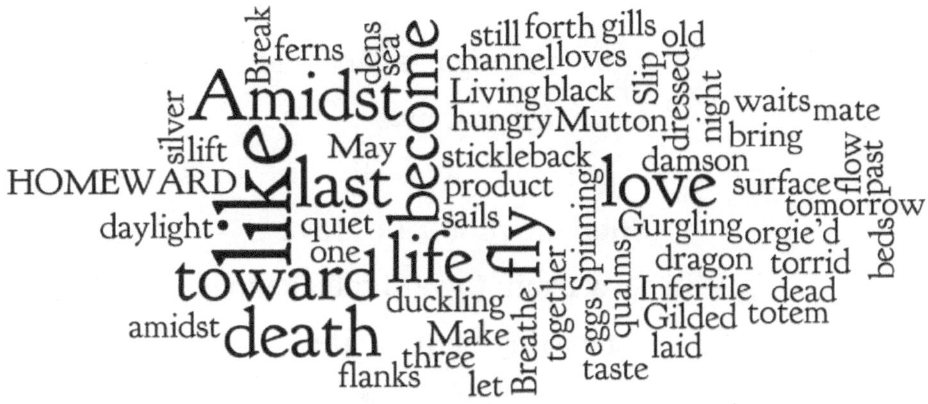

Mutton dressed as lamb

Is what I have become, is what I am, I am

Infertile as an old Swan

Sat on cold eggs

Deceived by my instinct for life

I have become again

The ugly duckling, and

Sit laughed at

Amidst

Kingfishers sounding like

Living car alarms

Who have no qualms

In swallowing the three spine stickleback

Snatched from torrid trout waters
Full of orgie'd scales
And whispered lovers lies
Of a better tomorrow

Yet quivering against her flanks
He still dies

Soon the product of love
Will flow again toward the channel
Feasting on new life
From above, and
Seen from above
Feathery gills let the mayflower
Breathe and beguile the hungry newborn
Slipping the surface tension to fly and
Mate amidst the dead on treetop oaks
While damson and the dragon fly
Spinning like silver balls in the sunshine's
Disco-dappled daylight
Make love hearts beneath
Gurgling
Green
Glowing
Gilded
Glades

In this late evening
Amidst the quiet dens of feathered ferns
Lilting like lavender laid away in papered drawers
Badgers bring bluebells home for beds, and
Dance around the totem pole of May
All together
In black and white
No smell of death,
No taste of night

It is time for me to go, at last
To lift the anchor of the past
To fill my sails with one last, great, breath, and
Cross the waiting Loch of death, and
Slip toward the open sea
The vastness of eternity
That waits to view my bobbing bow
Break forth on loves horizon now

-----O-----

PREAMBLE |

Those who are planted in the house of the LORD, Shall flourish in the courts of our God. They shall still bear fruit in old age; They shall be fresh and flourishing, To declare that the LORD is upright; He is my rock, and there is no unrighteousness in Him. (Ps 92:13-15 NKJV)

EXPLANATION |

I watched a television nature program, about trout, set in a river in the very heart of England. The descriptive language of everything in and around this water of life, was just....well it was just edible! Filmed in the spring time, everything was evocative of growth and change. It made me sad about getting old. This however, is not my river. There is a river I read, whose streams make glad the city of God. O Lord, take me there!

PERFORMANCE TIPS |

With a misery that turns to despondency and then quiet happiness!

| 26-66 | VOL 01 | [i]SLAPPER GLORIOUS

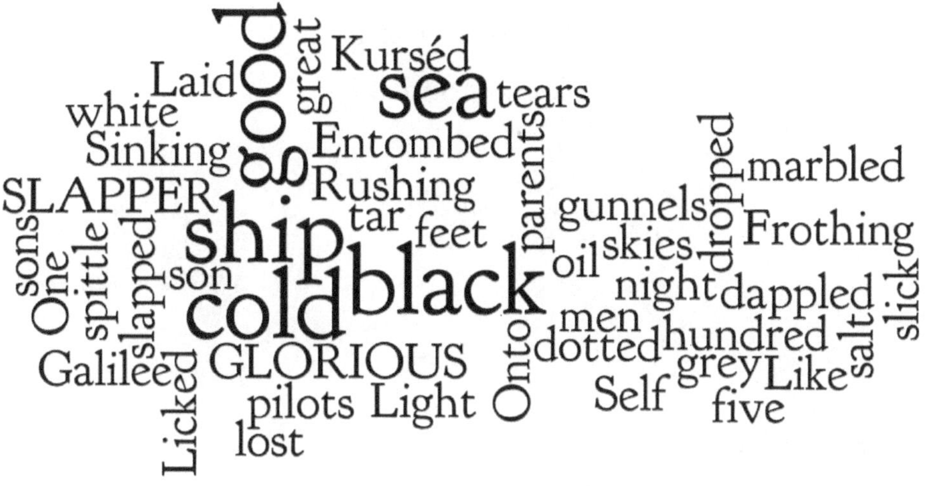

The sea

A great oil slick

Under grey, and dappled, marbled skies

Like cold black tar

Licked the gunnels of the good ship

"Light of Galilee"

Who slapped by pilots men again

Laid spittle

Frothing white

Onto the dotted black of night

And dropped salt tears

One for each lost son

And so, for all sons

Rushing

Sinking

Entombed, five hundred feet

Under a cold [ii]parents sea

In the Kurséd

Not so good ship

Self

-----*O*-----

PREAMBLE |

Then some began to spit on Him, and to blindfold Him, and to beat Him, and to say to Him, "Prophesy!" And the officers struck Him with the palms of their hands. Now as Peter was below in the courtyard, one of the servant girls of the high priest came. And when she saw Peter warming himself, she looked at him and said, "You also were with Jesus of Nazareth." But he denied it, saying, "I neither know nor understand what you are saying." And he went out on the porch, and a rooster crowed. (Mark 14:65-68 NKJV)

EXPLANATION |

I wrote this poem when sailing into St Malo with some friends. The news had just come over the radio of another sunk Russian submarine. This was one the world knew about. There are many they do not.

I used to be a Nuclear Submariner, serving in the 10th Submariner squadron out of Faslane. I was sailing into St Malo, many years later when the over the radio, the news was broadcast about the sunk Russian submarine the Kirsk, and the men trapped therein. They were never rescued; these fathers, these husbands, these sons, these young lost men. The sky was gun metal grey, when we sailed into the harbor. The sea was dark, my heart was heavy. I heard the noises from another submarine sunk many years before, and the tap tap tapping in Morse code which read over and over again……. "Is there any hope?" "Is there any hope?" "Is there any hope?" "Is there any hope?" "Is there any hope?" "Is there any hope?" "Is there any hope?" "Is there any hope?".

PERFORMANCE TIPS |

I am not sure this is a performance piece.....

[i] Slapper- A promiscuous and vulgar woman, a prostitute. Selfishness turns us into the sellers of self. Indeed, we pimp ourselves in the expression of our selfishness.

[ii] This is a play on words. The submarine went down in the Barents sea I believe.

| 27-66 | VOL 01 | THE SON-SHINE DAY!

It was a day like any other
The sun shone.

To tell his need the yapping puppy
Barked his master up to grudging early feed
And purring, creeping cat meowed to tell his need
Of milk, whilst winding his way
Around stumbling morning legs
That step to feed reluctant children
Shaken from deep sleepiness
To stare with squinting eyes
On black pans spitting sizzling eggs.

It was a day like any other

The sun shone.

A great day for a wedding!

With fresh and fragrant flowers
That perfumes the waking house
With sprinkling fragrant showers
From the button holes of men
Dressed as tightly suited gibbons
To old ladies swept with rouge
And bright red satin ribbons
With a black chimney sweep
And decorated Daimler
To match the sounding bells
With the blushes that should shame her.

For today the bride wears mocking white,
But that's alright.
Today.

It was a day like any other.
The sun shone.

The banquet was filled with giggling runny children
Cool sons, shy daughters flirting
Old men drinking and winking
And hard young men, drinking hard

Dodging judging looks from young mothers
Tired of chasing kids and husbands,
And after all that's said
Tired of losing.
And too late to warn the newly wed.

It was a day like any other
The sun shone.

The top table chilled by nerves
That might kill them
In delivering speeches to hearers that would neither
Move them nor thrill them
Only sit down with relief to be branded a bore!
For they've heard it
They've heard it
Heard it all, all before.
And at the end of the proceeding they all lift their thankful glass up
And proceed to the much talked of
Riotous booze up

It was a day like any other.
The sun shone.

And then GOD STOOD!

And thus the Son at His right hand
And all heaven stirred with the brush of bowing wings
"It is time!" He said,
"The fullness has come
Let the gatherers collect the tares and wheat,
Let the shepherds separate the goats and sheep,
Free the horsemen into this night,
And bring my Son in shining white
Glorify and lift Him high
See the name stamped on His thigh!
See His sword and praise the good
For today this blade will bathe in blood."

"Enough!" He roared
And shook the heavens to stars a falling
As from the outer edges
[i]Named by him they hear Him calling
And as a garment that is rolled away
They gather at the dawn
Of this His day.

It was a day like no other.

The Son shone.
In His strength.

-----O-----

PREAMBLE |

In My Father's house are many mansions; if it were not so, I would have told you. I go to prepare a place for you. And if I go and prepare a place for you, I will come again and receive you to Myself; that where I am, there you may be also. (John 14:1-3 NKJV)

EXPLANATION |

I have been to many weddings. This is typical British one! But one day.

PERFORMANCE TIPS |

With verve and gusto, holding a glass of something in your hand!

-----O-----

---

[i] CS Lewes - CHAPTER XIV - Night Falls on Narnia- - from 'The Last Battle' "He went to the Door and they all followed him. He raised his head and roared "Now it is time!" then louder "Time!"; then so loud that it could have shaken the stars, "TIME." The Door flew open. They all stood beside Aslan, on his right side, and looked through the open doorway. The bonfire had gone out. On the earth all was blackness: in fact you could not have told that you were looking into a wood, if you had not seen where the dark shapes of the trees ended and the stars began. But when Aslan had roared yet again, out on their left they saw another black shape. That is, they saw another patch where there were no stars: and the patch rose up higher and higher and became the shape of a man, the hugest of all giants. They all knew Narnia well enough to work out where he must be standing. He must be on the high moorlands that stretch away to the North beyond the River Shribble. Then Jill and Eustace remembered how once long ago, in the deep caves beneath those moors, they had seen a great giant asleep and been told that his name was Father Time, and that he would wake on the day the world ended.

"Yes," said Aslan, though they had not spoken. "While he lay dreaming his name was Time. Now that he is awake he will have a new one."

Then the great giant raised a horn to his mouth. They could see this by the change of the black shape he made against the stars. After that—quite a bit later, because sound travels so slowly—they heard the sound of the horn: high and terrible, yet of a strange, deadly beauty.

Immediately the sky became full of shooting stars. Even one shooting star is a fine thing to see; but these were dozens, and then scores, and then hundreds, till it was like silver rain: and it went on and on. And when it had gone on for some while, one or two of them began to think that there was another dark shape against the sky as well as the giant's. It was in a different place, right overhead, up in the very roof of the sky as you might call it. "Perhaps it is a cloud," thought Edmund. At any rate, there were no stars there: just blackness. But all around, the downpour of stars went on. And then the starless patch began to grow, spreading further and further out from the centre of the sky. And presently a quarter of the whole sky was black, and then a half, and at last the rain of shooting stars was going on only low down near the horizon.

With a thrill of wonder (and there was some terror in it too) they all suddenly realized what was happening. The spreading blackness was not a cloud at all: it was simply emptiness. The black part of the sky was the part in which there were no stars left. All the stars were falling: Aslan had called them home.

| 28-66 | VOL 01 | [i]BATHROOM BLESSINGS

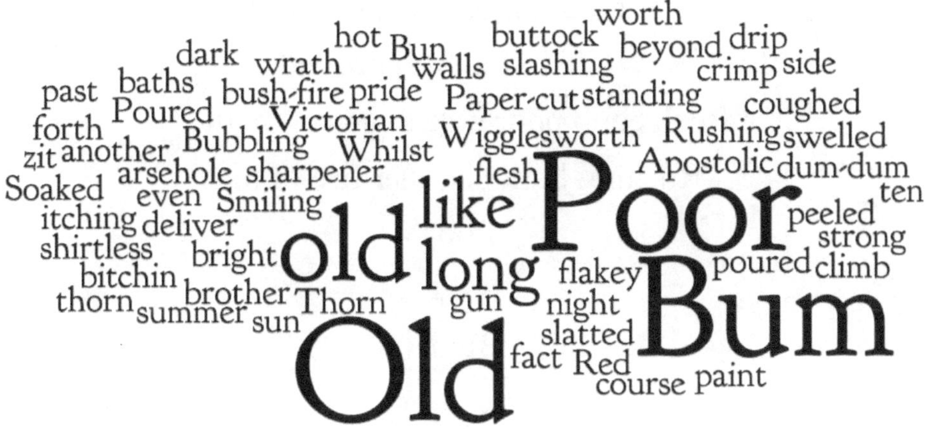

I have coughed myself another arsehole!
Leaving the sides of my sad sphincter
Bubbling like peeled paint on an old slatted door
Soaked long in the strong summer sun
Oh! The Stanley knife slashing and
Bad mouthed bitchin' that
Poured forth from the all the
Paper-cut itching of me
Poor
Old
Bum.

For what it's worth, even [ii]Wigglesworth
Suffered long with such Satanic fruit

Smiling and standing in Victorian crimp,
All pencil sharpener tight
Whilst each night healing a son, a brother,
A daughter and a mum
While in the background,
Beelzebub poured fire-ant oil on the
Rushing buttock bush-fire of his
Poor
Old
Bum.

A thorn in the flesh was not Peter's but Paul's
Another messenger of Old Red sent to buffet his balls
Lest he be swelled beyond measure and climb up the walls
Of pride, only to drip like watered down icing off
A hot
Cross
Bun
For in the Greek, of course, this past perfect
'Thorn in his side'
Was in fact the 'backside' of a well scratched,
Poor old
Apostolic
Bum.

So, who dares lay hold of my own grapes of wrath?
To deliver me from the ten zillion zit baths

Of all my Krakatoa days and
My stone-still restless, shirtless, shitless nights
Where I pray for the dum-dum of a dark suppository
To be Fired from the muzzle of an old iron
Cold barrel'd gun
Up the screaming bright red flaming passage of
My old and very flakey
Poor
Old
Achy
Bum

-----O-----

PREAMBLE |

And he came to the sheepcotes by the way, where was a cave; and Saul went in to cover his feet: and David and his men remained in the sides of the cave. (1 Sam 24:3 KJV)

EXPLANATION |

I drive a lot. I mean thousands of miles. Nuff said. Paul no doubt had some similar problems, especially from off of those cold cell floors and stone seats. An anal fissure led me to have an operation. It's a funny story really, because to help the fissure heal they break the muscles of the sphincter. Now, whilst also sporting my first dislocated septum from boxing, I decided to have both done at the same time. I think the surgeons were bored that day and swapped jobs! The ENT guy did my backside and the Proctologist worked on my nose. Sigh....The point is that disciples of Jesus do have the grapes of wrath to deal with even after they get saved! Get real please.

PERFORMANCE TIPS |

This can only be done in a pub! I find it best to perform this whilst sitting on a rubber ring or perched up on one buttock.

---

[i] Wikipedia says, Asher yatzar (Hebrew: ברכת) אשר יצר) "Who [has] formed [man(kind)]") is a blessing in Judaism. It is traditionally recited after engaging in an act of excretion, but is also included in many Jewish prayer books as a part of daily prayer prior to Birkat HaShachar. The purpose of this blessing is to thank God for good health. It expresses thanks for having the ability to excrete, for without it existence would be impossible. Though recited normally by observant Jews each time excretory functions are used, hence giving it the name the "bathroom blessing", it is also recited during the Shacharit service due to its spiritual significance to Jews. Humans are made in God's image, so it is an expression of awe toward God's creations.

[ii] Smith Wigglesworth was converted at age 8 in a Wesleyan Methodist revival, and an Anglican bishop confirmed him 2 years later. A Plymouth Brethren friend gave him instruction in the Bible. With their radical view of faith, the Brethren encouraged those involved in the Lord's work to simply pray and trust God for material needs. This meant that sharing one's needs publicly could only indicate unbelief. In his early years, the internationally acclaimed George Muller, another product of the Brethren, modelled the idealized "faith life" at his orphanage in Bristol. Without advertising the financial needs for the care of several thousand children, God miraculously provided. The fame of Muller may have inspired Wigglesworth. Although he said he read only the Bible, it is likely that the influence of the Brethren laid the seeds for his later confidence in the "prayer of faith" (James 5:15).

In his late teens in Bradford, England, while preparing to become a master plumber, Wigglesworth became attracted to the Salvation Army because they seemed to have more spiritual power than any other group. And through this association, he met Polly Featherstone. Subsequent to their marriage in 1882, they shared in ministry by opening Bowland Street Mission in Bradford.

Visiting nearby Leeds, he attended a "divine healing service" and became convinced from Scripture that God still heals the sick. Polly accompanied him to one of the services and received a healing herself. Wigglesworth, however, continued to suffer from haemorrhoids and took salts every day to clear his lower digestive tract. When Polly challenged him with his own unbelief, he anointed himself with oil according to the instruction in James 5:14. Instantly, healing took place and the malady never returned.

(5)

The settled blind mice
Fatted sleek and nice
Can never do wrong
Asleep in a praise song

(6)

Black the cliffs of Dover
The harvest now over
Shivering angels weep
As long the church doth sleep

(7)

Look now! The fields are rotten

The words of God forgotten
Beyond the ripe and ruin
Just a broken pot to poo in

(8)

Behold Thy slaughtered saints O Lord
Martyred, murdered with gun and sword
Avenge O God their shattered bones
Rebuild O God their broken homes

(9)

Dig their ashes in the potash ground
Re-route their blood to the Plymouth sound
Unfurl their sail and mocking pennant
Remove that rotting sitting tenant

(10)

Through revolution and through civil war
Let's remove that pink anti-Christian whore
Confident, fearless, and strong in the word
Let's cleanse our lost land of these vicious turds

-----O-----

PREAMBLE |

'These things says the Amen, the Faithful and True Witness, the Beginning of the creation of God: "I know your works, that you are neither cold nor hot. I could wish you were cold or hot. So then,

because you are lukewarm, and neither cold nor hot, I will vomit you out of My mouth. Because you say, 'I am rich, have become wealthy, and have need of nothing' — and do not know that you are wretched, miserable, poor, blind, and naked — I counsel you to buy from Me gold refined in the fire, that you may be rich; and white garments, that you may be clothed, that the shame of your nakedness may not be revealed; and anoint your eyes with eye salve, that you may see. As many as I love, I rebuke and chasten. Therefore be zealous and repent. Behold, I stand at the door and knock. If anyone hears My voice and opens the door, I will come in to him and dine with him, and he with Me. To him who overcomes I will grant to sit with Me on My throne, as I also overcame and sat down with My Father on His throne. "He who has an ear, let him hear what the Spirit says to the churches."""(Rev 3:14-22 NKJV)

EXPLANATION |

This is a piece which increases in 'syllabalic' force with each stanza. It as a call to the legacy church to have a revolution. Though I can see no one with balls big enough to count the cost in having one.

PERFORMANCE TIPS |

Be Cromwell addressing parliament.

-----O-----

| 30-66 | VOL 01 | THE UNFOUND GOD

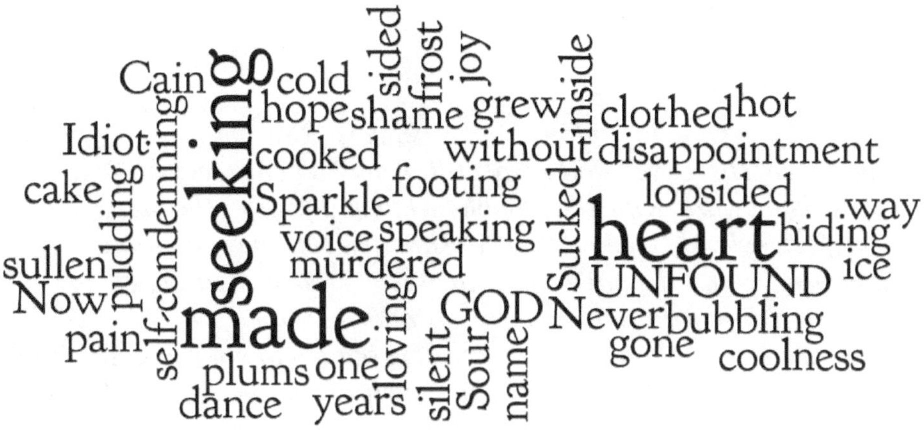

When for years the silent hiding
Sucked my seeking into shame
My self-condemning voice made ‘Idiot’ my name
Then the coolness of your heart grew frost inside my footing
And cooked an ice cold cake;
Sour plums without hot pudding.
So, sullen disappointment clothed my heart in pain
Now I’ve murdered all my hope and gone the way of Cain
For all lopsided loving and all one sided seeking
Never made a bubbling joy dance and
Sparkle in the speaking

-----O-----

PREAMBLE |

"Look, I go forward, but He is not there, and backward, but I cannot perceive Him; When He works on the left hand, I cannot behold Him; when He turns to the right hand, I cannot see Him. (Job 23:8-9 NKJV)

EXPLANATION |

I began by trying to follow Shakespeare's Rhyming scheme in his Sonnet, 'To His Love' and also utilize his 'When, then, so and for,' Stanza framework with the double whammy finish. He managed 14 lines of ten syllable each with a constant AB scheme repetition. It's all rather marvelous. I ended up with this! I have maintained the AB scheme, followed the When, then, so and for,' and created a double chiasm with a double whammy summary, but could not recreate his ten syllable lines. I have had to change the shape of the poem to better fit the format of this book and the text size. You get the picture anyways yes?

PERFORMANCE TIPS |

Be disappointed and questioning. This is only part of Job's statement however. Have this tang in your voice as you speak these words:

"Look, I go forward, but He is not there,
And backward, but I cannot perceive Him;
When He works on the left hand, I cannot behold Him;
When He turns to the right hand, I cannot see Him.
But He knows the way that I take;
When He has tested me, I shall come forth as gold.
My foot has held fast to His steps;
I have kept His way and not turned aside.
I have not departed from the commandment of His lips;
I have treasured the words of His mouth
More than my necessary food.
(Job 23:8-12 NKJV)

-----O-----

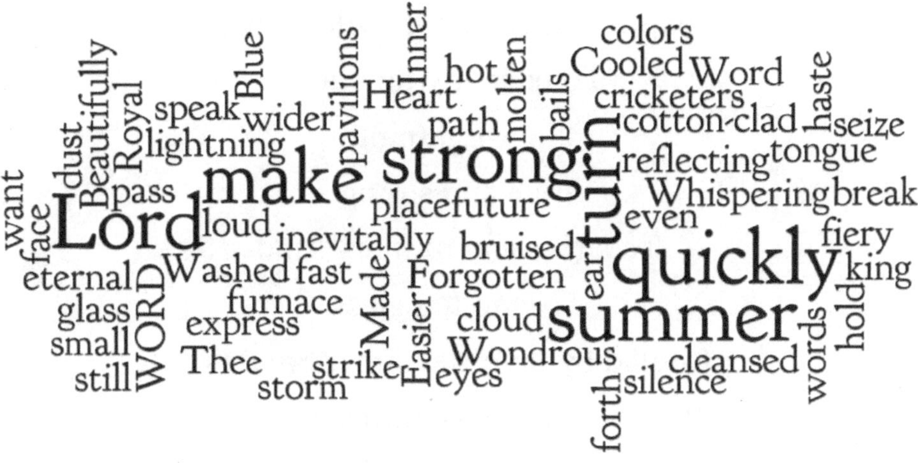

I want not to pass this place O Lord
As a small dust cloud
On a hot and dried out path
Leading nowhere
Save inevitably
To the end

[i]Forgotten.

Nor in silence hold this face O Lord but as loud
As a summer storm breaks quickly on cotton-clad cricketers
Snatching at the [ii]bails of life
Trying to make haste, even
To make fast their

Inner [iii]pavilions
Let me break forth and be!
To speak to hearts of men
To express the inexpressible, and then
To have my tongue
Fork lightning
Blue and strong
To strike and turn dry sand
To [iv]molten glass
Cooled by love's summer breezes
Replete with fiery furnace colors
Refracting and reflecting
The Royal purples of the eternal king
Beautifully bruised
To present me
Bountifully cleansed
[v]Washed by words
Made strong and stronger
Heart wide and wider still
Easier to seize my ear
In future whispers heard
[vi]To quickly turn all eyes to Thee
The [vii]Wondrous
[viii]Whispering
Word

-----O-----

PREAMBLE |

"And the angel of the LORD came back the second time, and touched him, and said, "Arise and eat, because the journey is too great for you. So he arose, and ate and drank; and he went in the strength of that food forty days and forty nights as far as Horeb, the mountain of God. And there he went into a cave, and spent the night in that place; and behold, the word of the LORD came to him, and He said to him, "What are you doing here, Elijah?" So he said, "I have been very zealous for the LORD God of hosts; for the children of Israel have forsaken Your covenant, torn down Your altars, and killed Your prophets with the sword. I alone am left; and they seek to take my life." Then He said, "Go out, and stand on the mountain before the LORD." And behold, the LORD passed by, and a great and strong wind tore into the mountains and broke the rocks in pieces before the LORD, but the LORD was not in the wind; and after the wind an earthquake, but the LORD was not in the earthquake; and after the earthquake a fire, but the LORD was not in the fire; and after the fire a still small voice. (1 Kings 19:7-12 NKJV)

EXPLANATION |

Now you will forgive me I hope for recording such a long quote from the Bible to begin with. You see, it is important to me personally that you see the context for this poem, and for my particular poetic voice in the coming 366 Poems, for I truly believe that God speaks more in whispers than in shouts and more in our hearts than in our heads. My personal coming to Him was because of the insistence of that same still small voice that moved with power within my spirit, within my soul, to finally and irresistibly draw me to Himself. An old fashioned truth for nowadays it would appear but still true never the less.

Unfortunately for some, this still small voice has made me want to shout!

PERFORMANCE TIPS |

To be said with Gusto! (and if he's not around then you are on your own.)

-----O-----

---

i Isaiah 40:6 The voice said, "Cry out!" And he said, "What shall I cry?" "All flesh is grass, And all its loveliness is like the flower of the field." NKJV

ii I used to be a wicket keeper, the most dangerous place in Cricket! For my American friends however, I do promise that I will not even attempt to explain the wonders of the second most boring game on the planet, baseball being the first of course!

So, now that I have offended a very large percentage of you, let me just say that in Cricket, on top of the three stump wicket (are you with me now) are two small pieces of wood called 'bails'. The falling, or violent removal of these bails by a cricket ball indicates that the batter is out! Anyway, enough, suffice to say that if it starts throwing it down with rain on an England summer's afternoon, and it surely will, then the white cotton clad cricketers will snatch the bails and take them indoors. Congratulations my good American friends, you are now better educated!

iii All Cricket grounds have a place to change, to store their gear, drink beer, allow teenagers to have their first illicit gropes and of course, shelter from English summer storms. These places are called Cricket Pavilions.

iv I'm pretty sure that it's in the Film 'Sweet Home Alabama' where the main character uses lightning rods to catch lightening from the thunder-headed clouds to produce glass for his factory.

v Ephesians 5:25-27 says: Husbands, love your wives, just as Christ also loved the church and gave Himself for her, that He might sanctify and cleanse her with the washing of water by the word, that He might present her to Himself a glorious church, not having spot or wrinkle or any such thing, but that she should be holy and without blemish. NKJV

vi It is interesting that the Word of God is heard and the heart is arrested so that the eyes might then truly see. The Biblical connection between words and spiritual vision is profound. Words are in the end paintings, videos, projections of the speaker on the walls of the hearing heart. I love how Spurgeon, that renowned 'Prince of Preachers', records his own testimony of coming to Jesus. Listen to what he says:

I sometimes think I might have been in darkness and despair until now, had it not been for the goodness of God in sending a snowstorm one Sunday morning, while I was going to a certain place of worship. I turned down a side street, and came to a little Primitive Methodist Church. In that chapel there may have been a dozen or fifteen people. I had heard of the Primitive Methodists, how they sang so loudly that they made people's heads ache; but that did not matter to me. I wanted to know how I might be saved....

The minister did not come that morning; he was snowed up, I suppose. At last a very thin-looking man, a shoemaker, or tailor, or something of that sort, went up into the pulpit to preach. Now it is well that preachers be instructed, but this man was really stupid. He was obliged to stick to his text, for the simple reason that he had little else to say. The text was—"LOOK UNTO ME, AND BE YE SAVED, ALL THE ENDS OF THE EARTH" (Isa. 45:22)

He did not even pronounce the words rightly, but that did not matter. There was, I thought, a glimmer of hope for me in that text.

The preacher began thus: "This is a very simple text indeed. It says 'Look.' Now lookin' don't take a deal of pain. It aint liftin' your foot or your finger; it is just 'Look.' Well, a man needn't go to College to learn to look. You may be the biggest fool, and yet you can look. A man needn't be worth a thousand a year to look. Anyone can look; even a child can look.

"But then the text says, 'Look unto Me.' Ay!" he said in broad Essex, "many on ye are lookin' to yourselves, but it's no use lookin' there. You'll never find any comfort in yourselves. Some say look to God the Father. No, look to Him by-and-by. Jesus Christ says, 'Look unto Me.' Some on ye say 'We must wait for the Spirit's workin.' You have no business with that just now. Look to Christ. The text says, 'Look unto Me.' "

Then the good man followed up his text in this way: "Look unto Me; I am sweatin' great drops of blood. Look unto Me; I am hangin' on the cross. Look unto Me, I am dead and buried. Look unto Me; I rise again. Look unto Me; I ascend to Heaven. Look unto Me; I am sitting at the Father's right hand. O poor sinner, look unto Me! Look unto Me!"

When he had . . . . managed to spin out about ten minutes or so, he was at the end of his tether. Then he looked at me under the gallery, and I daresay with so few present, he knew me to be a stranger.

Just fixing his eyes on me, as if he knew all my heart, he said, "Young man, you look very miserable." Well, I did, but I had not been accustomed to have remarks made from the pulpit on my personal appearance before. However, it was a good blow, struck right home. He continued, "And you will always be miserable—miserable in life and miserable in death—if you don't obey my text; but if you obey now, this moment, you will be saved." Then lifting up his hands, he shouted, as only a Primitive Methodist could do, "Young man, look to Jesus Christ. Look! Look! Look! You have nothing to do but look and live!"

I saw at once the way of salvation. I know not what else he said—I did not take much notice of it—I was so possessed with that one thought . . . . I had been waiting to do fifty things, but when I heard that word, "Look!" what a charming word it seemed to me. Oh! I looked until I could almost have looked my eyes away.

Now, isn't that a most marvellous testimony! The Holy Spirit's whisper brought Spurgeon to despair, the Father's providence brought him to the chapel, the preached Word boomed in his heart and called Him to Christ and in that calling Spurgeon looked until he could almost have 'looked his eyes away' and was at that moment, saved. The rest is history. In the Scriptures, ears and eyes go together like a good cheese and a great red wine.

vii Judges 13:17-18 Then Manoah said to the Angel of the LORD, "What is Your name, that when Your words come to pass we may honor You?" And the Angel of the LORD said to him, "Why do you ask My name , seeing it is wonderful ?"

Isaiah 9:6 For unto us a Child is born, Unto us a Son is given; And the government will be upon His shoulder. And His name will be called Wonderful ……….NKJV

viii 1 Kings 19:11-12 says: Then He said, "Go out, and stand on the mountain before the LORD." And behold, the LORD passed by, and a great and strong wind tore into the mountains and broke the rocks in pieces before the LORD, but the LORD was not in the wind; and after the wind an earthquake, but the LORD was not in the earthquake; and after the earthquake a fire, but the LORD was not in the fire; and after the fire a still small voice. NKJV

Job 26:4-14 says: To whom have you uttered words? And whose spirit came from you? "The dead tremble, Those under the waters and those inhabiting them. Sheol is naked before Him, And Destruction has no covering. He stretches out the north over empty space; He hangs the earth on nothing. He binds up the water in His thick clouds, Yet the clouds are not broken under it. He covers the face of His throne, And spreads His cloud over it. He drew a circular horizon on the face of the waters, At the boundary of light and darkness. The pillars of heaven tremble, And are astonished at His rebuke. He stirs up the sea with His power, And by His understanding He breaks up the storm. By His Spirit He adorned the heavens; His hand pierced the fleeing serpent. Indeed, these are the mere edges of His ways, And how small a whisper we hear of Him! But the thunder of His power who can understand?" NKJV

That still small voice heard by Elijah the prophet was the same voice that brought me to Jesus on August 28th 1979 when I was a young sailor on HMSM Renown refitting in Rosyth in the Kingdom of Fife. It was the little statement of 'how small a whisper we hear of Him' followed by the sound of 'thunder of His power' which both turned my eyes to Him and then years later, also propelled me into the ministry of Bible Teaching through WhisperingWord and all things Sixty Six.

| 32-66 | VOL 01 | I49 & OTHER ROADS

Reckless Rednecks on I49

Barefoot children at the Five & Dime

Black men shakin’, slidin’ skin

Pick-up trucks with nothin’ in

An extra syllable in evr’y vowel

Sealed flannel sheets and fresh-up towels

De-caff coffee

Diet coke

Well-dressed Christians and a hairy goat

Grits with jelly in the Waffle House

Crushed armadillo and a white wooden house

[i]Skeeter bugs a-dancing on black-eyed peas

Wal Mart

K-Mart

Plastic cheese
Plates that are full with more and more
Dirt in the corners at the [ii]Piggly Wiggly store
Strange verbal pointers to a guy called Booodah
Sweet & Low as a substitute for sugar
Porches full of rockers and swinging chairs
Blue perm rinses
Nasal hairs
Bland white cream on pecan pies
[iii]Hell mad preachers, all wearing ties
Lightest blues
Largest skies
Darkest cheeks
Whitest eyes

De-caff, diet
Racial riot
‘[iv]Look Out’ mountain
What a si-yat

[v]Hillary being pilloried in pounding pulpits
Passion for possession of presidential pundits
AN [vi]ELEPHANT, AN ELEPHANT,
A SMALL PINK PIG
Small English people where everything is big
White-collar necks that [vii]don’t give a fig
Don’t give a fig for a [viii]hot cross bun

Don’t give a fig for a man without a gun
For a man without a gun
Ain’t got no stature
A man without a gun
Don’t like [ix]Mrs. Thatcher
Mrs. Thatcher, Mrs. Thatcher
What a gal!
Ronny Reagan what a pal!
England and America
Bonded ties
England and America
Don’t tell lies
Don’t tell lies about [x]dogs in prison
Don’t tell lies about any ‘ism’
Socialism
Communism
[xi]Baptist schism
Split apart
Break my heart
Separation
Desolation

Bringing down of [xii]evil nation
Evil nation, makes you think!
Blacks and white are on the brink
Ice rink, blue ink, kitchen sink

[xiii]Presidents that cause a stink

High and mighty you may frown

[xiv]I WILL BRING YOU DOWN

-----O-----

PREAMBLE |

Your fierceness has deceived you, The pride of your heart, O you who dwell in the clefts of the rock, who hold the height of the hill! Though you make your nest as high as the eagle, I will bring you down from there," says the Lord. (Jer 49:16 NKJV)

EXPLANATION |

We have some good friends that live just off the interstate I75 in Byron Georgia. Byron was growing real fast the last time I visited and unfortunately and inevitably was being polluted with the same infectious food chains and shops that with the viciousness of a Spanish Flu epidemic are rapidly spreading all over America. Even so, Byron is still an interesting place and you still have travel along I49 to get there.

This performance piece is just a connection of observations about America, my adopted home and the place I love, especially the South. Like America, it is first a poem of contrast; racially, politically and culturally. Secondly and most importantly though, this piece is a warning for each and every one of us, against that dreaded complacency that comes with a fullness, which is fueled by a fat and forgetful arrogance.

PERFORMANCE TIPS |

If you dare, try to speak with a Southern United States accent of some of these delightful Dixie-like words. Indeed, some of these words are so onomatopoeic that they are just fun to say out loud and need saying in the sound they make. 'Slidin; skin' for example is like a slow slip handshake, take your time with these kind of words and you will feel the action and also communicate it well. Again this poem has a 2/4 beat and needs a lot of breath.

Now, imagine you are riding to the top of a roller coaster. Got it? Well the words 'Lightest blues Largest skies Darkest cheeks Whitest eyes- need to be said as slow and as expectantly as the last few yards at the top of the mechanized pull up. Then, 'De-caff, diet Racial riot Look Out' mountain What a si-yat' need to be said as though the Roller Coaster car is high above the ground on an flat even surface building up speed as it approaches its first enormous plummet. Take a very deep breath here before 'Hillary' (as recommended by most Republicans) and then enjoy the ride. Everything comes to a clattering halt at 'Presidents that cause a stink (well they would wouldn't they' and the last two words are said slowly and deliberately.

---

i For my British readers, this reference is to Mosquitoes! Nasty little buggers and the South has lots of them. I am at this moment, sat on a Kentucky Knob, editing this poem and itching madly from at least fifteen bites on my legs from Skeeters and Chiggers. Chiggers? You do not want to know!

ii For my British readers I have to tell you that yes, there are a chain of stores in the South called Piggly Wiggly! I can only imagine the first board meeting in someone's kitchen or old barn or even a smoky old bar where the founding executives, some good old boys maybe with farmer's tans, sat down and discussed what to name this new enterprise and after a few shots of white lightning came up with the forward thinking name of 'Piggly Wiggly'.

"Yes sir", said Goober Bouhger, "Piggly Wiggly! Catchy name. I like it! Boy I'll tell you whurt, we're a gonna make a barrel load a money on that bad boy name. Yes siree, whoooeeee, Piggly Wiggly, shut yer mouth and slap yer grandma!"

The name Piggly Wiggly really sets the tone for the whole mess of stores. Cheap, run down, dirty, plastic and nasty. Tell you what though, if you haven't got a lot of money and work in a chicken factory in the Mountains of North Georgia, then Piggly Wiggly is a veritable God send. The last one I went to was in fact across the road from a Chicken factory in Ellijay, North Georgia in one of those same mountain towns. It was right next to the consignment shop that sold junk to support a home for fleeing battered women of husbands who drank too much, treated them no better than their hound dogs and couldn't get a job at the chicken factory across the road, which, just to show the greasier side of life, left a layer of fine mist of chicken fat slippy-ness in the parking lot and an odour in the entrance of the Piggly Wiggly store that smelled like the devil's underpants after a long weekend of sinning.

iii The South of course is full of Bible-buckle, Bible-belt independent fundamentalism. I am a fundamentalist with my emphasis laying on the fun, rather than on the damn mental. You know what I mean. Jesus spoke more about hell than anyone and certainly in His earthly ministry, spoke more about hell than heaven. However, He wasn't wearing a suit and tie and 'spittin in yer' eye while slamming down His fist on an old wooden pulpit, His badly tied tie, hanging from a fat neck and draped over a bulbous belly that has spent far too many Sunday afternoons in 'Shoneys.' No, when Jesus spoke of hell, He wasn't self-righteous, no siree, He spoke about hell in very angry terms, to the self-righteous, I say especially to the religious self-righteous! Tight neck ties make self-righteous preachers even fatter and redder than they were before. Maybe they should be banned from the . (No, I am not talking about the neck ties!)

iv Look Out Mountain in Chattanooga.

v 'Hitllary' Clinton. Of course!

vi Southern Democrats were once the South's popular Christian Party. Now, to be a Democrat, is to be thoroughly associated with the devil! I was once fired from a Romanian Baptist church in South Florida because I said you could be a Christian and vote Democrat. Those were the days before I knew better. (Only kidding. You can be a Democrat if you are a Christian. But you still 'aint right.

vii Fig leaves, were of course supposedly first used to cover up Adam and Eve's unmentionables! So if you don't give a fig…well, it means you don't really care. At all! You don't give a fig.

viii In old Christian countries Good Friday saw the baking of Buns with a cross marked on their tops. White collar workers, the rising professional class of America, don't really care for the old fashioned Easter Gospel or any of its traditions. And Oh yes, Bun rhymes with gun!

ix Ah, The Thatcher Reagan years. What a beautiful mess.

x There are always 'dog's in prison.' 'Extraordinary rendition' has of course now been legalized in offshore illegal dog pounds. Though Obama says he's going to shut down 'Gitmo'.

xi The preferred Baptist way of Church planting.

xii Which Empire proved to be maybe most evil in the years following the cold war end?

xiii The Clintons again.

xiv God's vow in how He shall crush the rising up of Lucifer, that old light of the morning, and anyone, thing or nation, motivated, activated, sanctioned or certified by him. Jer 49:16 "O you who dwell in the clefts of the rock, Who hold the height of the hill! Though you make your nest as high as the eagle, I will bring you down from there," says the LORD" NKJV

| 33-66 | VOL 01 | THE NEW RECRUIT

Why this clanking armor

That limits my expression,

Why this [i]sharpened two-edged sword

Cast in the armory of heaven?

[ii]Why this binding helmet

That sweats my head and chaffs my neck,

Why these studded sandals

Which bind me to the deck?

Why this giant's shield

And tightened belt around my waist?

Why this clamorous dressing

Why LORD, all this haste?!

Why this shiny breast-plate

So heavy that my legs bend?

[iii]"Stand up!" He snapped
"Right quickly now
For I'll teach you to [iv]fight [v]legends."

"I didn't join for all this bother
Nor heavy armored [vi]clobber,
I joined for sweet security
Peace, love, joy, altogether."

"Fight or die.
Be overrun
Your life be in subjection.
Or stand,
And grasp
These charméd tools
I provide for your protection.
For the waves that hit you now my son
Are small as is the [vii]din,
For these are only battles messengers
From massing on the rim.
Legions vile,
With power replete
Make haste to come and storm you,
So stand up straight!
And listen hard,
Or soon they'll all be o'er you.

Your transfer friend was sealed in blood
Your former master [viii]angered,
And soon these fiends of hell my son
Would have your soul endangered.
[ix]Your eyes
Your mind
Your touch
Your taste
All gateways to your soulish heart,
Shall be accosted by the foulest fiends
With desire to tear apart.

This is a work that I have started.
It is a work of manly errands.
So stand up my son
Right quickly now
For [x]I must teach you
To fight legends."

-----*O*-----

PREAMBLE |

"Behold, I have created the blacksmith Who blows the coals in the fire, Who brings forth an instrument for his work; And I have created the spoiler to destroy. No weapon formed against you shall prosper, And every tongue which rises against you in judgment You shall condemn. This is the heritage of the servants of the LORD,

And their righteousness is from Me," Says the LORD (Isa 54:16-17 NKJV)

EXPLANATION |

I remember being a new recruit myself in the Royal Navy being guided through a scary part of training entitled NBCD. (Nuclear, Biological and Chemical Defense) Like most young men I joined the Royal Navy for the wonderful uniform and it was indeed a magnificent uniform once, before the Ministry of Defense saw Velcro and Polyester as a new recruiting tool! Idiots! Anyhoo, the NBCD suit was hot, cumbersome and full of packets of needles filled with unknown poisons to inject yourself with, if ever the ships citadel was breached. I remember thinking "I never joined up for this!" I tell you that I have had that same thoughts many times since I joined the massed ranks of Jesus Christ the Lord!.

PERFORMANCE TIPS |

To be said with two voices. Fear and Trembling in both of them. The recruit and the Master Sergeant.

-----O-----

---

i Heb 4:12 For the word of God is living and powerful, and sharper than any two-edged sword, piercing even to the division of soul and spirit, and of joints and marrow, and is a Discerner of the thoughts and intents of the heart. NKJV

ii Eph 6:11-18 Put on the whole armor of God , that you may be able to stand against the Wiles of the devil.

For we do not wrestle against flesh and blood, but against principalities, against powers, against the rulers of the darkness of this age, against spiritual hosts of wickedness in the heavenly places.

Therefore take up the whole armor of God , that you may be able to withstand in the evil day, and having done all, to stand.

Stand therefore, having girded your waist with truth, having put on the breastplate of righteousness,

and having shod your feet with the preparation of the gospel of peace;

above all, taking the shield of faith with which you will be able to quench all the fiery Darts of the wicked one.

And take the helmet of salvation, and the sword of the Spirit, which is the word of God;

praying always with all prayer and supplication in the Spirit, being watchful to this end with all perseverance and supplication for all the saints –NKJV

iii If you've been in the Armed forces, I mean the real ones, way back, when men were men and boys were frightened, then you will no doubt remember the very tough, stern and often abusive Sergeant Majors and or, Royal Navy Parade Ground Instructors! The molding of pimply boys into a fighting machine is a serious task and demands a fervent firmness. Honestly we kid ourselves if we do not see this life saving and attitude as one aspect of the character of God the Holy Spirit. "I'm your mother now lad!" Can you hear Him?

iv "I must teach you to fight legends!" I believe I got this little phrase from one of my favorite and in my opinions one the greatest Science Fiction series ever produced, Babylon 5. Despite its predictable humanistic and arrogant ending, it remains for me an epic adventure story not just about the control of the universe by either the Vorlons or the Shadows, but a true representation of the eternal conflict between light and darkness. Babylon 5, I love it!

v Eph 6:12 For we do not wrestle against flesh and blood, but against principalities, against powers, against the rulers of the darkness of this age, against spiritual hosts of wickedness in the heavenly places. NKJV

Make no mistake about it, these ancient adversaries have names, capacities, histories and battle honors amongst their own hosts. Evil entities have been around a long time and are despicable legends in their own ranks and in our own histories as well. It is these forces, which we battle against.

vi Clothes.

vii Noise, clamor.

viii 'Christians' fight with Appolyon as described by John Bunyan in Pilgrims progress tells of Satan's mad anger against those of us redeemed from his grasp. Listen-

'So he went on, and Apollyon met him. Now the monster was hideous to behold:

he was clothed with scales like a fish, and they are his pride; he had wings like a dragon, and feet like a bear, and out of his belly came fire and smoke; and his mouth was as the mouth of a lion. When he was come up to Christian, he beheld him with a disdainful countenance, and thus began to question him.

APOL. Whence came you, and whither are you bound?

CHR. I am come from the city of Destruction, which is the place of all evil, and I am going to the city of Zion.

APOL. By this I perceive thou art one of my subjects; for all that country is mine, and I am the prince and god of it. How is it, then, that thou hast run away from thy king? Were it not that I hope thou mayest do me more service, I would strike thee now at one blow to the ground.

CHR. I was, indeed, born in your dominions, but your service was hard, and your wages such as a man could not live on; for the wages of sin is death, Rom. 6:23; therefore, when I was come to years, I did, as other considerate persons do, look out if perhaps I might mend myself.

APOL. There is no prince that will thus lightly lose his subjects, neither will I as yet lose thee; but since thou complainest of thy service and wages, be content to go back, and what our country will afford I do here promise to give thee.

CHR. But I have let myself to another, even to the King of princes; and how can I with fairness go back with thee?

APOL. Thou hast done in this according to the proverb, "changed a bad for a worse;" but it is ordinary for those that have professed themselves his servants, after a while to give him the slip, and return again to me. Do thou so to, and all shall be well.

CHR. I have given him my faith, and sworn my allegiance to him; how then can I go back from this, and not be hanged as a traitor.

APOL. Thou didst the same by me, and yet I am willing to pass by all, if now thou wilt yet turn again and go back.

CHR. What I promised thee was in my non-age: and besides, I count that the Prince, under whose banner I now stand, is able to absolve me, yea, and to pardon also what I did as to my compliance with thee. And besides, O thou destroying Apollyon, to speak truth, I like his service, his wages, his servants, his government, his company, and country, better than thine; therefore leave off to persuade me farther: I am his servant, and I will follow him.

APOL. Consider again, when thou art in cool blood, what thou art like to meet with in the way that thou goest. Thou knowest that for the most part his servants come to an ill end, because they are transgressors against me and my ways. How many of them have been put to shameful deaths! And besides, thou countest his service better than mine; whereas he never yet came from the place where he is, to deliver any that served him out of their enemies' hands: but as for me, how many times, as all the world very well knows, have I delivered, either by power or fraud, those that have faithfully served me, from him and his, though taken by them! And so will I deliver thee.

CHR. His forbearing at present to deliver them, is on purpose to try their love, whether they will cleave to him to the end: and as for the ill end thou sayest they come to, that is most glorious in their account. For, for present deliverance, they do not much expect it; for they stay for their glory; and then they shall have it, when their Prince comes in his and the glory of the angels.

APOL. Thou hast already been unfaithful in thy service to him; and how dost thou think to receive wages of him?

CHR. Wherein, O Apollyon, have I been unfaithful to him?

APOL. Thou didst faint at first setting out, when thou wast almost choked in the gulf of Despond. Thou didst attempt wrong ways to be rid of thy burden, whereas thou shouldst have stayed till thy Prince had taken it off. Thou didst sinfully sleep, and lose thy choice things. Thou wast almost persuaded also to go back at the sight of the lions. And when thou talkest of thy journey, and of what thou hast seen and heard, thou art inwardly desirous of vainglory in all that thou sayest or doest.

CHR. All this is true, and much more which thou hast left out; but the Prince whom I serve and honor is merciful, and ready to forgive. But besides, these infirmities possessed me in thy country, for there I sucked them in, and I have groaned under them, been sorry for them, and have obtained pardon of my Prince.

APOL. Then Apollyon broke out into a grievous rage, saying, I am an enemy to this Prince; I hate his person, his laws, and people: I am come out on purpose to withstand thee.

CHR. Apollyon, beware what you do, for I am in the King's highway, the way of holiness; therefore take heed to yourself.

APOL. Then Apollyon straddled quite over the whole breadth of the way, and said, I am void of fear in this matter. Prepare thyself to die; for I swear by my infernal den, that thou shalt go no farther: here will I spill thy soul. And with that he threw a flaming dart at his breast; but Christian had a shield in his hand, with which he caught it, and so prevented the danger of that.

Then did Christian draw, for he saw it was time to bestir him; and Apollyon as fast made at him, throwing darts as thick as hail; by the which, notwithstanding all that Christian could do to avoid it, Apollyon wounded him in his head, his hand, and foot. This made Christian give a little back: Apollyon, therefore, followed his work amain, and Christian again took courage, and resisted as manfully as he could. This sore combat lasted for above half a day, even till Christian was almost quite spent: for you must know, that Christian, by reason of his wounds, must needs grow weaker and weaker.

Then Apollyon, espying his opportunity, began to gather up close to Christian, and wrestling with him, gave him a dreadful fall; and with that Christian's sword flew out of his hand. Then said Apollyon, I am sure of thee now: and with that he had almost pressed him to death, so that Christian began to despair of life. But, as God would have it, while Apollyon was fetching his last blow, thereby to make a full end of this good man, Christian nimbly reached out his hand for his sword, and caught it, saying, Rejoice not against me, O mine enemy: when I fall, I shall arise, **Mic. 7:8;** and with that gave him a deadly thrust, which made him give back, as one that had received his mortal wound. Christian perceiving that, made at him again, saying, Nay, in all these things we are more than conquerors, through Him that loved us. **Rom. 8:37.** And with that Apollyon spread forth his dragon wings, and sped him away, that Christian saw him no more. **James 4:7.**

In this combat no man can imagine, unless he had seen and heard, as I did, what yelling and hideous roaring Apollyon made all the time of the fight; he spake like a dragon: and on the other side, what sighs and groans burst from Christian's heart. I never saw him all the while give so much as one pleasant look, till he perceived he had wounded Apollyon with his two-edged sword; then, indeed, he did smile, and look upward! But it was the dreadfullest sight that ever I saw.

So when the battle was over, Christian said, I will here give thanks to him that hath delivered me out of the mouth of the lion, to him that did help me against Apollyon. And so he did, saying,

"Great Beelzebub, the captain of this fiend,

Designed my ruin; therefore to this end

He sent him harness'd out; and he, with rage

That hellish was, did fiercely me engage:

But blessed Michael helped me, and I,

By dint of sword, did quickly make him fly:

Therefore to Him let me give lasting praise,

And thank and bless his holy name always." '

ix This time I recommend a thorough reading of John Bunyans “Holy War” where he describes the enemies attack against the eye gate and the ear gate etc, of our very own citadel. What a Pastor he was! What a writer and what a true Curer of Souls he has remained throughout the centuries.

x I wish to God, that the ‘old lady’ spirit of the church, was finally cast out and that pastors would indeed begin to teach their flock to fight legends.

| 34-66 | VOL 01 | THE CLAIMING

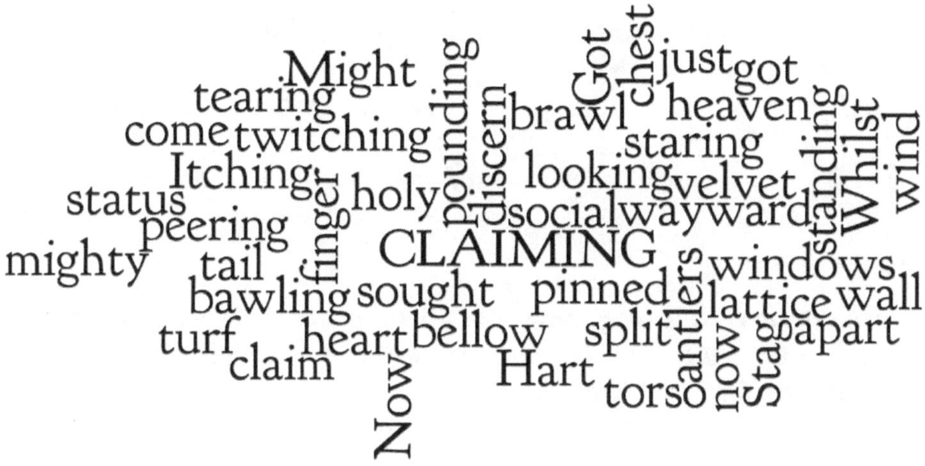

The Stag has sought me out, and
Now is standing by my wall, and
His mighty velvet antlers are now
Itching for a brawl, and
He's looking through my windows, and
He's peering through my lattice, and
He's staring at my finger
To discern my [i]social status, for
Whilst tearing up my turf
His tail is twitching in the wind, and
The [ii]bellow of His bawling
Has got me up and
Got me pinned, and
The pounding in my torso

Might just split my chest apart

For this [iii]Hart of holy heaven
Has come to claim my wayward heart

-----O-----

PREAMBLE |

My beloved is like a gazelle or a young stag. Behold, he stands behind our wall; He is looking through the windows, Gazing through the lattice. My beloved spoke, and said to me: "Rise up, my love, my fair one, And come away. (Song of Solomon 2:9-10 NKJV)

EXPLANATION |

I have heard this verse unpacked and applied in so many ways over the years. Yet, the core of it I believe is one of unstoppable desire. Jesus truly is the hound of heaven pursuing those He loves, and communicating in the terms of the desire for wedding night fulfilment, no other picture will do here to convey His desire to be with us His church and us as individual parts of this is His bride. Now that's amazing.

I want the encouraging focus of this poem to be the time of union. God is unstoppable in His desire to know us. I know! That pictures a little too uncomfortable to grasp, never the less, it is true. The foundation of the piece is from an ancient erotic love poem. Of course its spiritual, BUT it is also erotic, breathless and full of desire...

PERFORMANCE TIPS |

I would read the Scripture verse out loud, then perform the piece with breathlessness, back against a wall, hiding. Like a poorly clothed Adam amongst the green leaved trees.

-----O-----

---

[i] Ring Finger. Wedding band.

[ii] Mating call.

[iii] The Male Red Deer is referred to as an 'Hart' rather than a Stag.

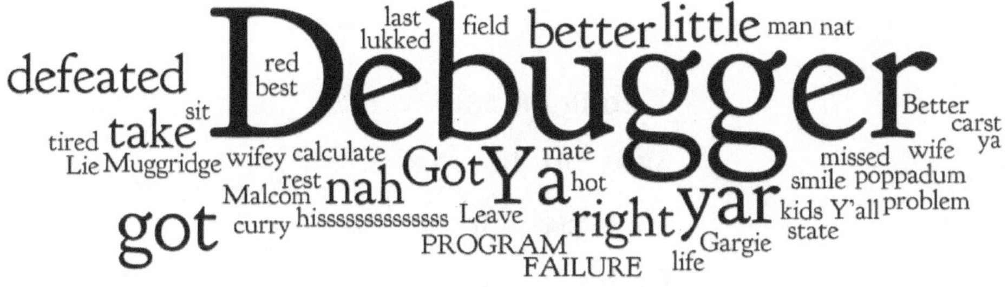

Debugger said to me
Ya' got a problem man
[i]Ya' got your red hot curry
But ya' got no [ii]poppadum

Debugger said to me
[iii]Y'all tired and in a state
[iv]Got no little wifey
Got no little mate

Debugger said to me
[v]Ya nah it all is last
Better sit right down nah
And calculate the carst

Debugger said to me
Lie down and take a rest
[vi]It defeated [vii]Malcom Muggridge
It defeated [viii]Gargie best

Debugger said to me
Why not take yar life
Be better for yar kids
Be better for yar wife

Debugger said to me
Leave the field you'll nat be missed
Debugger lukked at me
And smile right through his [ix]hisssssssssssss

-----O-----

PREAMBLE |

So the great dragon was cast out, that serpent of old, called the Devil and Satan, who deceives the whole world; he was cast to the earth, and his angels were cast out with him. Then I heard a loud voice saying in heaven," Now salvation, and strength, and the kingdom of our God, and the power of His Christ have come, for the accuser of our brethren, who accused them before our God day and night, has been cast down. (Rev 12:9-10 NKJV)

EXPLANATION |

You need four things to understand this poem. First, I wonder if you have ever had a time on your computer when a program has failed and a dialogue box has then miraculously appeared asking if you would like to run the Debugger? In other words, it would like to run another program you won't understand to help find the problem you didn't understand that made your program with all the data you really needed, CRASH! If you have a Microsoft operating system, I know this rarely happens to you, so use your imagination here! OK, so you have run the debug program and now know at least where the failure occurred. You now have some information to give to the experts, those pimply little, greasy little geeks, down at Best Buys. Secondly, in England the word 'Bugger' used in this context has reference to an incredulous malevolence. Thirdly, this needs to be read with a 'Bangladeshi English' or better still, a Jamaican accent. Fourthly, fourthly, the devil, that ancient old bugger, wants you dead. He will kill you if he can, but will take more joy in you doing the job for him. Do not listen to him..

PERFORMANCE TIPS |

This needs to be read with a Bangladeshi English or better still, a Jamaican accent.

-----O-----

---

i The First cut of the evil one is "Yes you've got that, but you haven't got this and this is what makes that worth something, worth anything, worthless, without it."

ii A paper-thin pancake, grilled or fried till crisp, served with Indian dishes. Probably from Tamil 'poppatam', or perhaps from 'paruppa atam' which means lentil cake. In any event, you can't have a good curry without a poppadum, it's unheard of!

iii The Second cut of the evil one is "You can't handle this can you?"

iv The Third cut of the the evil one is "You are all alone in this. Always have been, always will be."

v The Fourth cut of the evil one is "it's not worth going on. Calculate it, it's not worth it."

vi We've all got an 'IT'. What's yours?

vii The Enigmatic Malcom Muggeridge dismayed many Evangelicals when his spiritual evolution turned him into a Roman Catholic!

viii His country and most Brits regarded George Best as the greatest footballer ever! He died in 2005 of alcohol related issues. Concerning his sport, his was a wasted life.

ix Rev 20:2 He laid hold of the dragon, that serpent of old , who is the Devil and Satan, and bound him for a thousand years; NKJV

| 36-66 | VOL 01 | SODDEN HOMELESS

[i]The flowers of the forest are darker now
The soil has been drenched with blood
The new shoots of spring are colder now
The cloaked sun no longer warms the good
The silence of the night is broke with 'crack'ing now
The evil has left the pit to walk the darker wood
And the creatures lay like dead men now
To mind the menace if they could

For the voice of less Able yet cries with pain
Against the justifying of his cleaner brother, Cain
Who makes the tread of hills yet ever steeper
To deny that we are all,
Our brother's keeper.

-----O-----

PREAMBLE |

The poor man is hated even by his own neighbor, But the rich has many friends. He who despises his neighbor sins; But he who has mercy on the poor, happy is he. (Prov 14:20-21 NKJV)

EXPLANATION |

I remember being a commuter to the city of London, stepping off the Victoria train and making my way towards Buckingham gate and the High-Rise Plush offices in the early hours of the morning, the smelly drunks, still lying on their cardboard in their Hotel room doorways each morning. You could hear the Yuppies stepping over them spilling their morning Latte's "Soddin' Homeless. Bloody government, should do something about them" I'm sure they will. How a nation deals with it's homeless is a sure test as to its level of its good neighborliness. The housing crisis in Britain is a sodding disgrace!

PERFORMANCE TIPS |

Wear a bobble hat and sit in a sleeping bag. Bloody government. They are a bunch of Buffoons stoking the fires of the Big Issue. This really gets my goat.

---

i I remember this tune was played at a commemoration of the Falklands war dead. Many veterans end up homeless. The Flowers of the Forest should still be played for them. Wikipedia says the "Flowers of the Forest is an ancient Scottish folk tune. Although the original words are unknown, the melody was recorded in c. 1630 as part of the John Skene of Halyards Manuscript as "Flowers of the Forrest," though it's composition date is lost to the mists of time ---- Powerful solo bagpipe versions of the song are used at services of remembrance, funerals, and other occasions; many in the Commonwealth know the tune simply as "The Lament" which is played at Remembrance Day or Remembrance Sunday ceremonies to commemorate war dead.

The first verse of the song contrasts happier times with grief at the losses:

I've heard the lilting, at the yowe-milking,

Lasses a-lilting before dawn o' day;
But now they are moaning on ilka green loaning;
"The Flowers of the Forest are a' wede away".

Translating uncommon words, this could read:

I've heard the singing, at the ewe-milking,
Lasses a-singing before dawn of the day;
But now they are moaning on every milking-green;
"The Flowers of the Forest are all withered away".

| 37-66 | VOL 01 | TIMINGS

Jesus never comes too late
Jesus is never worried
Jesus never waits too long
Jesus is never hurried.

After all these years of impatient wait
My heart is full of anger
My fists are full of hate
So don't sing me the old, old song
That "Jesus never comes to late,
Jesus never waits too long."

Jesus never comes too late
Jesus is never worried

Jesus never waits too long
Jesus is never hurried.

My bills are beasts with popping raiment
Never full and always hurried
They grow bigger with each monthly payment
And I'm squashed and scared and worried,
So don't sing me the old, old song
"That Jesus never comes to late
That Jesus is never hurried."

Jesus never comes too late
Jesus is never worried
Jesus never waits too long
Jesus is never hurried.

My years have passed [i]"in this one thing",
My love is now the talked of sounding gong
I have lost the given voice to sing
For Jesus has waited too long, too long.
So don't sing me the old, old song
"That Jesus never comes too late
That Jesus is never wrong."

Jesus never comes too late
Jesus is never worried
Jesus never waits too long

Jesus is never hurried.

“[ii]A day with Me a thousand years
A thousand years a day
My plans stretch to eternity
My purpose not delayed
[iii]I see the start
I see the end
I see the working out.
[iv]All possibilities are there for Me to bring about.
None! I say, can stay my hand
Though many make a fuss
So hold on tight
My little child
And exercise some trust.
[v]I work all things e'en for your good
According to my purpose
No action breath or meanest move
Is wasted, bent or surplus
[vi]The keys of hell and death
Are hanging by My waist
I am the God who opens
And when I do, make haste!
And I am the God of slamming door
Of creaking closing gate
So be sure, I am never hurried.

So be sure, I am never late.

Hush then my silly one
[vii]Lest My anger should grow hotter
Is this how earth red clay
Should speak to Heaven's Potter?
I use as
I choose as
I do as
I will.
I do
When I will
I do
Where I will.
I am the horses of Israel's chariot
Un-reigned I ride out
E'en to [viii]Judas Iscariot
To [ix]Pilot, and [x]Dothan, to Naomi's Mara
To [xi]Job and to [xii]John Mark
To [xiii]Annanias and Saphira
In the end friend,
Mark well,
[xiv]I shall face all who slight Me
And then they shall know Me
The Lord God Almighty!

Be still all ye nations

Ye waves, be calmed before Me
[xv]Kneel, kiss the Son
And for His mercies implore Me.
Mercies, yes these, for your sojourn you mourn
Yet as night meets the day they are fresh as the morn
Prepared in advance long before you were said
To ease your choiced path
And light the dark where you tread
E'en for these did I suffer
And rise from the dead.
Yet child there remains yet but one thing
In need and
One thing in must
That in faith
You stretch forth your hand
And lay hold in trust

For I tell you the truth;

Jesus never comes too late
Jesus is never worried
Jesus never waits too long
Jesus is never hurried.

-----O-----

PREAMBLE |

Then Jesus said to them plainly, "Lazarus is dead. And I am glad for your sakes that I was not there, that you may believe. Nevertheless let us go to him." Then Thomas, who is called the Twin, said to his fellow disciples, "Let us also go, that we may die with Him." (John 11:14-16 NKJV)

EXPLANATION |

This poem is like the book of Job in that it begins with a man arguing with his friends and end ups with God stepping in to finish the argument! When you are disappointed in waiting, the calm refrain of "Jesus never comes to late" (repeated beginning with and then repeated a further three times in this poem) is no comfort, especially when it is spoken from the comfortable lips of the settled. Keep up the bitterness though and keep up the argument, for you just might get God to step in and shut you up!

PERFORMANCE TIPS |

This is a two voice Poem...the First a mocking anger, even derisory , but most certainly disappointed voice. The second begins 'A day with Me a thousand years.' This is God's very niffed voice, speaking to and then beyond the first voice to all others who deride His times, purposes and ways.

---

i Mark 10:21 Then Jesus, looking at him, loved him, and said to him, "one thing you lack: Go your way, sell whatever you have and give to the poor, and you will have treasure in heaven; and come, take up the cross, and follow Me."NKJV

Luke 10:40-42 But Martha was distracted with much serving, and she approached Him and said, "Lord, do You not care that my sister has left me to serve alone? Therefore tell her to help me."

And Jesus answered and said to her, "Martha, Martha, you are worried and troubled about many things.

But one thing is needed, and Mary has chosen that good part, which will not be taken away from her."NKJV

ii 2 Peter 3:8-9 But, beloved, do not forget this one thing, that with the Lord one day is as a thousand years , and a thousand years as one day .

The Lord is not slack concerning His promise, as some count slackness, but is longsuffering toward us, not willing that any should perish but that all should come to repentance. NKJV

iii Rev 21:3-7 And I heard a loud voice from heaven saying, "Behold, the tabernacle of God is with men, and He will dwell with them, and they shall be His people. God Himself will be with them and be their God.

And God will wipe away every tear from their eyes; there shall be no more death, nor sorrow, nor crying. There shall be no more pain, for the former things have passed away."

Then He who sat on the throne said, "Behold, I make all things new." And He said to me, "Write, for these words are true and faithful."

And He said to me,"It is done! I am the Alpha and the Omega, the Beginning and the End. I will give of the fountain of the water of life freely to him who thirsts.

He who overcomes shall inherit all things, and I will be his God and he shall be My son. NKJV

iv 1 Sam 23:7-13 And Saul was told that David had gone to Keilah. So Saul said, "God has delivered him into my hand, for he has shut himself in by entering a town that has gates and bars ."

Then Saul called all the people together for war, to go down to Keilah to besiege David and his men.

When David knew that Saul plotted evil against him, he said to Abiathar the priest, "Bring the ephod here."

Then David said, "O LORD God of Israel, Your servant has certainly heard that Saul seeks to come to Keilah to destroy the city for my sake.

Will the men of Keilah deliver me into his hand? Will Saul come down, as Your servant has heard? O LORD God of Israel, I pray, tell Your servant." And the LORD said, "He will come down."

Then David said, "Will the men of Keilah deliver me and my men into the hand of Saul?" And the LORD said, "They will deliver you."

So David and his men, about six hundred, arose and departed from Keilah and went wherever they could go. Then it was told Saul that David had escaped from Keilah; so he halted the expedition. NKJV

v Rom 8:28 And we know that all things work together for good to those who love God, to those who are the called according to His purpose. NKJV vi Rev 1:17-18 And when I saw Him, I fell at His feet as dead. But He laid His right hand on me, saying to me, "Do not be afraid; I am the First and the Last.

I am He who lives, and was dead, and behold, I am alive forevermore. Amen. And I have the keys of Hades and of Death .NKJV

vii Rev 3:14-16 "And to the angel of the church of the Laodicean's write, 'These things says the Amen, the Faithful and True Witness, the Beginning of the creation of God:

"I know your works, that you are neither cold nor hot. I could wish you were cold or hot.

So then, because you are lukewarm, and neither cold nor hot, I will vomit you out of My mouth. NKJV

viii The betrayer of Jesus. One of HIS chosen disciples

ix Placed in power by God having his authority given to him by God. Yet he washed his hands of the Son of God

x Joseph was sent to Dothan by his father to look for his brothers. It was from there that his brothers sold him into slavery.

xi Ask God to never mention your name to the Devil!

xii At one point in his life, John Mark deserted his mission and his companions

xiii Disciples who lied against the Holy Spirit and were killed by God. Called yet killed. Called yet killed!

xiv Phil 2:9-11 Therefore God also has highly exalted Him and given Him the name which is above every name, that at the name of Jesus every knee should bow, of those in heaven, and of those on earth, and of those under the earth, and that every tongue should confess that Jesus Christ is Lord, to the glory of God the Father. NKJV

xv Ps 2

Why do the nations rage, And the people plot a vain thing?

The kings of the earth set themselves, And the rulers take counsel together, Against the LORD and against His Anointed, saying,

"Let us break Their bonds in pieces And cast away Their cords from us."

He who sits in the heavens shall laugh; The LORD shall hold them in derision.

Then He shall speak to them in His wrath, And distress them in His deep displeasure:

"Yet I have set My King On My holy hill of Zion."

"I will declare the decree: The LORD has said to Me, 'You are My Son, Today I have begotten You.

Ask of Me, and I will give You The nations for Your inheritance, And the ends of the earth for Your possession.

You shall break them with a rod of iron; You shall dash them to pieces like a potter's vessel.'"

Now therefore, be wise, O kings; Be instructed, you judges of the earth.

Serve the LORD with fear, And rejoice with trembling.

Kiss the Son , lest He be angry, And you perish in the way, When His wrath is kindled but a little. Blessed are all those who put their trust in Him. NKJV

| 38-66 | VOL 01 | HE SAID WHAT?

Is this the thing He really meant?
When into wolves His sheep he sent
A pair of shoes an empty purse
A black and shiny flower-filled hearse?

Is this the thing He really meant
A comfort Zone of 10%
A cozy house and willing kids
Cool underpants without the skids?

Is this the thing He really meant
A life-time's debt to old cement
To turn sane salt and lovely light
To tasteless silent empty night?

Is this the thing He really meant?
[i]ISA's pensions endowment
[ii]Mission Praise on pale pink kneelers
[iii]A PCC of dirty dealers?

Is this the thing He really meant
A disassociate ornament
A religious face to fit my smiles on
In the petty precincts of plastic Zion?

Is this the thing He really meant
When into wolves His sheep he sent
A pair of shoes an empty purse
A black and shiny flower-filled hearse?

-----O-----

PREAMBLE |

Then the chief priests and the Pharisees gathered a council and said, "What shall we do? For this Man works many signs. If we let Him alone like this, everyone will believe in Him, and the Romans will come and take away both our place and nation." And one of them, Caiaphas, being high priest that year, said to them, "You know nothing at all, nor do you consider that it is expedient for us that one man should die for the people, and not that the whole nation should perish." Now this he did not say on his own authority; but being high priest that year he prophesied that Jesus would die for the nation.. (John 11:47-51 NKJV)

EXPLANATION |

Middle Class Christianity, the proud poodle of the professional classes, frowns on the abandoned life. They have reinterpreted the gospel demands to be applied only to those called to be stupid enough to step out in faith and abandon their roofs and their old age to God. This poem contains some hard questions for said Poodledum! Note now, people who live like this will only employ Pastors who justify and live the same lifestyle.

PERFORMANCE TIPS |

With middle class incredulity.

-----O-----

---

i "The individual savings account (Isa) was launched by the government to encourage people to save for the future. It is effectively a tax-efficient wrapper in which you can hold either stock market-based investments or a traditional savings account. As an incentive, any interest earned on savings or bonds and any capital gains made on investments held within an ISA are tax free. This is particularly good news for people on higher incomes who are taxed at the rate of 40% on all their savings and investment income."

ii Mission Praise is a hymn book used in a wide variety of churches, especially in Britain, including the Church of England. It currently contains 1144 hymns. It was revolutionary in the 1980's....but now.....not so revolutionary!

iii Wikipedia says that "The Parochial Church Council or PCC, is the executive body of a Church of England parish. It is constituted as a body corporate by the Church Representation Rules set out in Schedule 3 to the Synodical Government Measure 1969, and consists of the clergy and churchwardens of the parish, together with a number of representatives of the laity elected by the annual parochial church meeting of the parish. Its powers and duties are defined by certain Acts of Parliament and other legislation, principally the Parochial Church Councils (Powers) Measure 1956. It has the responsibility of co-operating with the incumbent (rector, vicar or priest) or priest in charge in promoting the mission of the Church in its parish. Formally, the PCC is responsible for the financial affairs of the Church and the care and maintenance of the church fabric and its contents. These latter responsibilities are executed by churchwardens. It also has a voice in the forms of Service used by the church and may make representations to the bishop on matters affecting the welfare of the parish."

I sat on a Deanery Synod once and subsequently on the PCC. What can I say! If you want to see Big Time politics played out on a small stage then join a PCC! Hilarious.

| 39-66 | VOL 01 | THE PILLSBURY DOUGH BOY

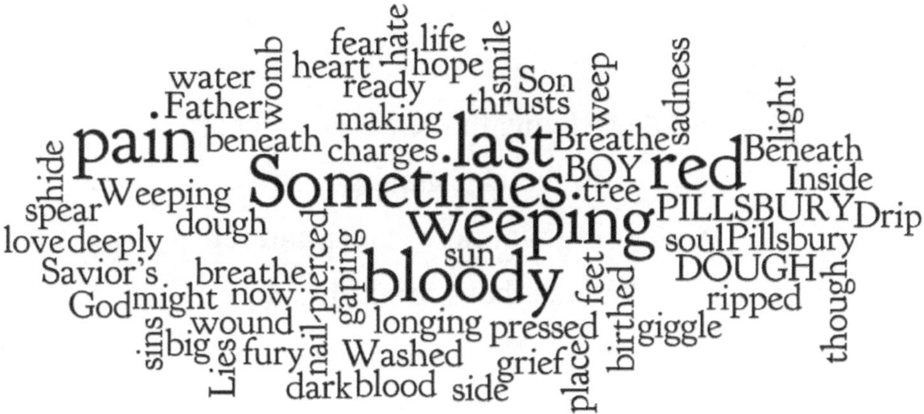

[i]Pillsbury dough pushed pain.
No smile or giggle though, but
The coming of a 'too big to be birthed' baby
Sometimes weeping
Sometimes longing to weep..

Breathe now, breathe deeply…..
"And where's the bloody Father?"
"He's with His bloody Son
Weeping at His feet
Beneath the dark red sun
As all the sins of time are pressed into His soul
As grief and pain and sadness

Drip down each nail-pierced hole"

And last of all, and last of all! My God!
In fury, hate and fear
It's me that charges at the tree
It's me that thrusts the spear
And there beneath the Savior's heart
A ripped and gaping side
A weeping wound of clear and red
A place that I might hide

Washed in water
Bathed in blood
Inside a womb of my own making
Lies life, and light and love and hope
All ready for the taking.

-----O-----

PREAMBLE |

But we see Jesus, who was made a little lower than the angels, for the suffering of death crowned with glory and honor, that He, by the grace of God, might taste death for everyone. Bringing Many Sons to Glory For it was fitting for Him, for whom are all things and by whom are all things, in bringing many sons to glory, to make the captain of their salvation perfect through sufferings. For both He who sanctifies and those who are being sanctified are all of one, for which reason He is not ashamed to call them brethren, saying: "I will declare Your name to My brethren; In the midst of the assembly I will sing praise to You." And again: "I will put My trust in Him."

And again: "Here am I and the children whom God has given Me." Inasmuch then as the children have partaken of flesh and blood, He Himself likewise shared in the same, that through death He might destroy him who had the power of death, that is, the devil, and release those who through fear of death were all their lifetime subject to bondage. (Heb 2:9-15 NKJV)

EXPLANATION |

(The final wound is always at our own hand and in entering into it we find life and the Savior's heart……………….. So I have heard).

Dealing with our sin, dealing with our baggage when it comes to the surface, can be such an emotional eruption that it is akin to giving birth! Many mothers, suffering in the delivery room, begging for a three punch combination of Demerol and an Epidural and a Pudenial block, all cry out in anger at the absent lover saying "Where's the bloody Father!" It's as though they are saying "Where is the person responsible for this present pain!"

In the same way, I have observed that Christians who are in fact giving birth to life, often go through great pain and in doing so follow their natural tendency in blaming God for everything. Here the question of the location of God in all of this is answered by the Holy Spirit reminding us of the location of the Father, which is with His Son, observing his suffering on our behalf. When we go there with the Father, eventually amongst the masses crying for the Son's crucifixion, amongst the close inflictors of such pain, we might just find ourselves as one of the instigators, one of the culprits even.

PERFORMANCE TIPS |

With doubt.

-----O-----

---

i It was Pillsbury Products that came up with their classic blue-eyed smiling little white dough boy, who giggled sweetly when you pressed in his tummy. Your tummy still gets pushed in by large invisible prodding fingers when emotional pain and poison is truly vomited from you, but there are no sweet giggles. Not yet anyways and sometimes not for a long time.

| 40-66 | VOL 01 | SWEET CHERRY PIE

On the modulated Tuning band
From the bearded braided Holy Land
Of gated ears and ready pen
A new voice is heard on
'WOW
FM'

Yes triple 7
'WOW
FM'
The voice of now the voice of then
Is pleased to introduce to you
The man with which you'll have to do
The man we love to

Squeeze us
Please us
That lovely cuddly sandaled Jesus
The Man of manna
Tease and toba
Wearing a shawl and a kinda o' toga
Will be pleased to make the feathers fly
As He cuts and serve us Cherry Pie
Oh Cherry pie
Sweet Cherry pie
His words will taste like
Cherry pie

Yeah flying out and
Coming at you
The man that ate you
Chewed and spat you
Big red words on white-washed walls
That had the guts
The heart the balls
To lift the lid on open graves
To raise the dead and calm the waves
To shine the light on things
That slither
That no nonsense
Jock
No lilley liver

Bowman lost without his quiver
No sharp pressed suit
No corporate tie
Just red and dripping Cherry Pie
Oh Cherry pie
Sweet Cherry pie
His words will taste like
Cherry pie

So tune up
Tune in to
'WOW
FM'
You'll never be the same again
Come hear Him love the leaping lame,
Snap the captive's bondage chain
Shake that box of wine so much
You'll leave yer chair your pain your crutch
He'll make you laugh He'll make you cry
He'll make you live He'll make you die
My
He'll lift yer head to God Most High!
He'll blot the sun
He'll dark the sky
He'll make the lover weep and sigh
He'll grasp your heart

He'll grip your thigh and
Speak of wine and
Cherry pie

Oh Cherry pie
Sweet Cherry pie
His words will taste like
Cherry pie
Oh Cherry pie
Sweet Cherry pie
His words will taste like
Cherry pie

"Jesus
Coming Soon
The Third day of Every week
On Triple 7
'WOW
FM'

-----O-----

PREAMBLE |

Brethren, do not be children in understanding; however, in malice be babes, but in understanding be mature. In the law it is written: "With men of other tongues and other lips I will speak to this people; And yet, for all that, they will not hear Me," says the Lord (1 Cor 14:20-21 NKJV)

EXPLANATION |

The other tongue here is the radio advertising tongue. I love American radio, especially on the quickly dying AM band.....great advertising!

PERFORMANCE TIPS |

Shout this one and spit it out! This is in effect, a commercial for Jerusalem's new and ultimate 'Shock Jock'. So when come to reading it, be sure to put on your most glitzy commercial voice that you can possibly muster! Be that Radio advertising Shock Jock! For me, I always say 'WOW FM' in a very different low voice.

| 41-66 | VOL 01 | IN MORNING'S MOUTH

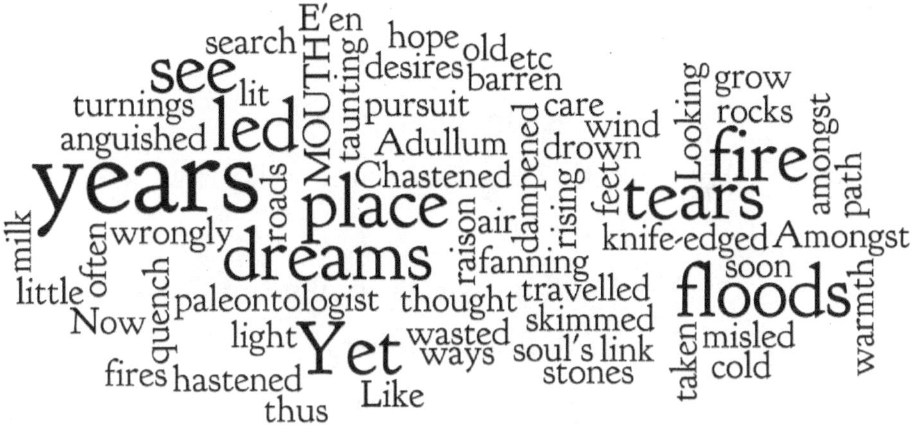

Now I see the place my dreams have led me.
To barren rocks and dampened air.
Have I lived in the light of my own fires
And thus am compassed by all care?
To search amongst these anguished tones
Like some old skimmed milk paleontologist
Looking for his missing link
Amongst the knife-edged stones

The ways I should have taken
The turnings
In pursuit of raison d'étre.
The roads I've wrongly travelled
The wasted years

The pain, etc.

Yet the fire is not yet out
E'en I often thought it so,
A little hope
A fanning wind
And soon this taunting flame will grow

Yet I will drown this rising fire
In floods of tears
In floods of tears
And I will quench my soul's desires
That through the years
That through the years
Has lit a path before
My hastened
Chastened feet
And in warmth has so misled me

For, in the cold of this Adullum

I now see the place my dreams have led me.

-----*O*-----

PREAMBLE |

Have mercy on me, O God, have mercy on me, for in you my soul takes refuge. I will take refuge in the shadow of your wings until the disaster has passed (Psalm 57:1 NKJV)

EXPLANATION |

This is a poem for the spiritually despondent. David named one of his Psalms to be sung as follows; For the director of music. To the tune "Do Not Destroy." Of David. A miktam. When he fled from Saul into the cave.!

PERFORMANCE TIPS |

With despondency.

-----O-----

| 42-66 | VOL 01 | FROZEN SOLID

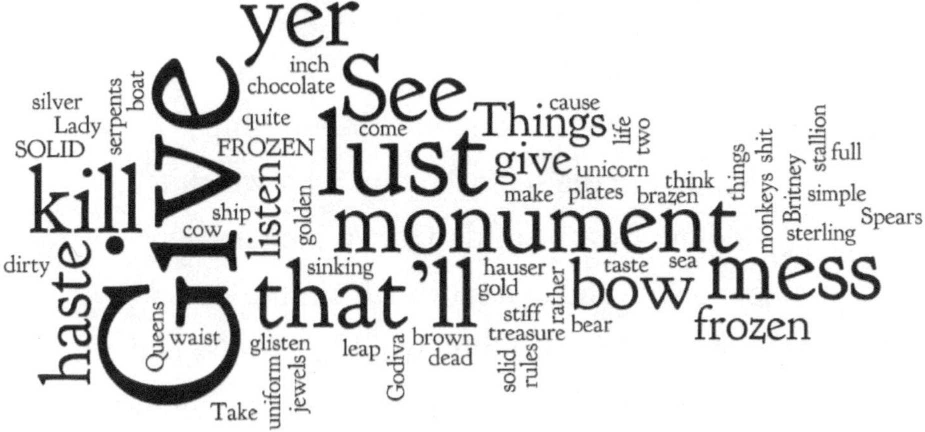

Give me money and give me jewels

Take from me duty and dirty rules

Give me gold the serpents hissen

Things that shine and things glisten

But no I will not, I will not listen,

No I will not, listen to you

Give me the lust of my saliva

Give me Britney Spears give me Lady Godiva

Give me Things quite to my taste

But No I will not, I will not haste,

No I will not, haste to you

Give to me a stallion or a unicorn

Give me china plates and The Queens uniform
Give me brazen monkeys or a golden cow
But no I will not, I will not bow,
No I will not, bow to you

See me leap from my sinking ship
See me in the sea of my own brown shit
See me frozen solid to a two inch hauser
See me stiff and dead through simple cause O
Wouldn't think ,Wouldn't bow wouldn't come make haste
But would rather bear my treasure in a frozen waist
A life boat of full of chocolate and sterling silver
A monument to mess and a lust that'll kill yer
A monument to mess and a lust that'll kill yer
A monument to mess and a lust that'll kill yer
A monument to mess and a lust that'll kill yer

-----O-----

PREAMBLE |

For thus says the Lord GOD, the Holy one of Israel: "In returning and rest you shall be saved; In quietness and confidence shall be your strength." But you would not (Isa 30:15 NKJV)

EXPLANATION |

Annie Dillard tells about some British explorers in their search for the North Pole in the 1800's. They knew it would be a two to three year journey, yet each sailing vessel carried only a twelve-day supply of coal. Instead of bringing more coal, each ship made room for 1,200 volume library, a hand organ playing 50 tunes, china place settings for officers and men, cut wine glass goblets, and sterling silver flatware. They carried no special clothing for the arctic except the uniforms of the Queen's navy. When the Eskimos came across their frozen remain, the men were all dressed up, pulling a lifeboat full of sterling silver and chocolate.

PERFORMANCE TIPS |

Every Stanza comes to a heavy snow bank stop. Let the last four lines be your trail off into becoming frozen solid.

-----O-----

| 43-66 | VOL 01 | VENI VIDI VICI

My Victorious Master

Vanquished every variety of

Vicious evil

Vaunted, flaunted

Undauntedly laid

By desperate men

Dastardly bastards and

Dreadful demons

Before His ever present

Mild and all mellifluous feet

Those cross squeezed out souls

Dripping with honey

Treading down the neck of all the

Squirming skubalac battalions

Who always press hard the damage
Against His loving chest
To trip and test, to trip and try
The all sufficiency of His ever fragrant
Myrrh perfumed
Milk-laden
Mighty breasts

No matter!

Monstrous evil's
Ever manifesting, always morphing face of
Bitter malevolence was still
Minimized to nothing-ness
With a Word from the Word

You losers all!

Look!
No loquacious sliding, slimey slipping or
Slope shouldering here
Just the gun-smoke smoldering of the
Word-gun of Heaven's King
Showing that just one bullet from His mouth
Biting the bullseye of the hideous heart
Was enough
Of a high calibraic

Dum-Dum for the Dumb-Dumb
To make the thing depart
Wounded
Bleeding
Running
Rage and filth
Darkness, madness, and all bondage of the broken heart
Condemnation, accusation, hideous guilt and consternation
Even the hunger of a soul left famished
All with a Word
Were sent off in shame
Banished
To the benches of the pit
Waiting for the game to end.

"Behold!
You running hounds
You mangy dogs of hell
Behold! You losers all
Behold! And mark you well,
For now raised above my battlements
Of my former life all squandered
There flies His blood red flag that reads
"I Came
I Saw
I Conquered!"

Now PISS OFF!

-----O-----

PREAMBLE |

Great multitudes followed Him, and He healed them all. (Matthew 12:15 NKJV)

EXPLANATION |

Veni Vidi Vici is quite simply a Prayer of Personal Exorcism. I knew of a family who moved to a new city and were so overcome with a spirit of fear, that they huddled on the bed together in their room, and it began to levitate. It was only when they told that spirit of fear to 'F' off in Jesus name that the bed fell with a bang to the floor and they got on with life. Sometimes, with as much respect as you can muster, you just have to tell the demons where to get off.

PERFORMANCE TIPS |

With a fearful defiance.

-----O-----

| 44-66 | VOL 01 | A DOUBLE CONE

Tiger skin. One user. Little blood.

Lion pelt. Humanely killed. Legal

Rhino horn for men

Monkey gland mix

Satisfaction Fixed.

Dicks.

Never seen the light of day

Babies heads. Unused with eyes.

Little toes, severed thighs

Murder, much misunderstood

Planned Parenthood.

Bastards.

-----O-----

PREAMBLE |

"The first of the first fruits of your land you shall bring to the house of the LORD your God. You shall not boil a young goat in its mother's milk." Ex 34:26 NKJV)

EXPLANATION |

This format uses 6 lines in a 6 ,5,4,3,2,1 WORD format. Ice cream poem poetry really, rather than choc-ice poetry. (Conical rather than square. More cold than delicious.) This however, is a double ice-cream poem. Anyway, I am waffling. Look, recently on the news it was reported that a bloody lion got killed in an illegal hunt and had some of its parts sold for, well, for medicine? Sexual enhancement maybe? Grrrr..... I am not for killing lions mind you, though to save their Albert, Mr. Ramsbottom would have blown its bloody head off if he had a gun. "The Magistrate gave his opinion that no one was really to blame, and he said that he hoped the Ramsbottoms, would have further sons to their name. At that Mother got proper blazing, "And thank you, sir, kindly," said she, "What, waste all our lives raising children, to feed ruddy Lions? Not me!" Wallace got away with it. Not Cecil.

What narked me was that the world seemed in uproar at Cecil the Lion getting his teethed pulled out by an overpaid dentist, while 70 million babies or more are murdered and their sucked out, well preserved body parts sold on by Planned bloody Parenthood.

So here are two conical poems. Enjoy.

PERFORMANCE TIPS |

Let each line be said form a different position. Let the last word come with spitting disdain.

| 45-66 | VOL 01 | SICK 66

Sacrificed wife on alter of ministry.
Manacled kids in handcuffs of respectability.
‘[i]Passed it on.’ Shelves now empty.
Preached vulnerability. [ii]Goolies now in neck.
Shagged [iii]Delilah. [iv]O why, O why?
Early Retirement. Selling temporal life insurance.

-----O-----

PREAMBLE |

For we are members of His body, of His flesh and of His bones. "For this reason a man shall leave his father and mother and be joined to his wife, and the two shall become one flesh." This is a great mystery, but I speak concerning Christ and the church.

Nevertheless let each one of you in particular so love his own wife as himself, and let the wife see that she respects her husband. Children, obey your parents in the Lord, for this is right. "Honor your father and mother," which is the first commandment with promise: "that it may be well with you and you may live long on the earth." (Eph 5:30-6:3 NKJV)

EXPLANATION |

Sick 66 or The Ballad of the Fallen Pastor.

This is poem of 6 words with 6 lines. Each six words should tell a story in intervals and the whole six lines interweave each one of them. One of the terms used for this method is 'Fast Fiction' supposedly born out of Hemmingway's drunken $10 challenge to write a novel with six words. Hemmingway apparently pocketed his winnings when he passed the napkin of the new novel around. It simple said, 'For sale. Baby shoes. Never worn.'

PERFORMANCE TIPS |

Nonchalantly

-----O-----

---

i Henry Burton, Pass It On

Have you had a kindness shown?
Pass it on;
'Twas not given for thee alone,
Pass it on;
Let it travel down the years,
Let it wipe another's tears,
'Til in Heaven the deed appears —
Pass it on.

ii British vulgar slang meaning testicles.

iii Delilah, that devil with breasts who sex slaved Samson to death.

iv : Tom Jones – 'Delilah' Lyrics

I saw the light on the night that I passed by her window
I saw the flickering shadow of love on her blind
She was my woman
As she deceived me I watched and went out of my mind

My my my Delilah
Why why why Delilah
I could see, that girl was no good for me
But I was lost like a slave that no man could free

At break of day when that man drove away I was waiting
I crossed the street to her house and she opened the door
She stood there laughing
I felt the knife in my hand and she laughed no more

My my my Delilah
Why why why Delilah
So before they come to break down the door
Forgive me Delilah I just couldn't take any more

She stood there laughing
I felt the knife in my hand and she laughed no more

My my my Delilah
Why why why Delilah
So before they come to break down the door
Forgive me Delilah I just couldn't take any more

Forgive me Delilah I just couldn't take any more

| 46-66 | VOL 01 | DANCES WITH ANGELS

I am English

A product of the visual imprint of choir stalls and

College boy 'hair-cutted' boys all

Dressed in little bright red cassocks

With a white frock on top

Singing angelically to one another

Across an empty space before a golden

Crossed alter lit by large white candles

All standing stiff and upright, rigid and immovable

As uncomfortable as their starched and stodgy underwear

Fearful to turn the page too quickly,

Too loudly, too noticeably

Steady boys…….Steady

True choirs of angels however must be Scots!
They must be slaves released and Maori black
Tattooed and tongue exposed
Forearm Clapping and thigh slappingly fearsome
Happy and horse like, neighing for battle
Hoofing the ground in foot stomping joy
Like the Zulus at [i]Rorke's Drift
Dancing on a pinhead of death
Uncaring if they fall in the dust
Just
Glad to be part of it all, and
Dancing

-----O-----

PREAMBLE |

What would you see in the Shulamite — As it were, the dance of the two camps? (Song of Solomon 6:13 NKJV)

O my love, you are as beautiful as Tirzah, Lovely as Jerusalem, Awesome as an army with banners! (Song of Solomon 6:4 NKJV)

How beautiful are your feet in sandals, O prince's daughter! The curves of your thighs are like jewels, The work of the hands of a skillful workman. (Song of Solomon 7:1 NKJV)

EXPLANATION |

The Song of Songs is many things and not least is the story of mad and almost maniacal sensual desire. Which, by the way, for a man in his fifties like me is pretty exhausting just to read about. Even so, the well-loved woman is enticed back by her beloved and his watching friends and all the other choral ladies, to come and display her all-consuming drop dead gorgeous beauty one more time. Without being pornographic, this is a call for an exclusively energetic and erotic encore. "What do you wanna see boys and girls?" she says, "The Dance of Two Camps?" Literally, DDG (Drop Dead Gorgeous), is here referring to 'the dance of Mahanaim'. Now this has reference to when Jacob, broken and fearful, returned to the place of his family and birth to meet what he fully expected to be the vengeful wrath of his long robbed brother Esau. Jacob thought he was going to be killed and that all he had and cared for would be taken, brutalised utilised and destroyed. To comfort his heart at that quaking time, God gave Jacob, his faith then faltering child, a vision of two camps of angels, two armies, two regiments of singing soldiers, two choirs of armed angels, all seemingly war dancing their way to his protection. Now there's a thought, I mean, do angels actually do the Maori Hakka?

So, anyway, Jacob, now partly pacified, went on his way, after the angels of God had met him, and Jacob said, "This is God's camp." And he called the name of that place Mahanaim, two camps. Genesis 32:1-2 NKJV

I wonder today if DDG today points us to what seemed to be a well-known dance now lost in the sands of time. A heavenly dance if you will, which was awesomely warlike, beautiful and glorious, joyous in expectancy, dangerous like a sword dance, and maybe as scary as a highland fling performed by a kilted Scots guardsman whirling like a whooping dervish whilst wearing no underwear! The dance of the 'meat and two veg' if you will! Maybe I go to far. My point is simple however: Real joy, deep joy, the ecstatic release of tension to peace, all leads to dancing. In the Holy Scriptures, the joy of reconciliation, of union, of redemption and of deliverance, of forgiveness and of blessing, always results in dancing, even if it does mean exposing your bits! So, without getting arrested please, I pray your joy will turn to dancing, and that God would grant you happy feet and two companies of kilted angels to teach you how to fling it about a bit. Oh and remember: ignore the daughters of Saul. They are always far too anal for their own good.

PERFORMANCE TIPS |

I think you should perform the [ii]Maori Haka whilst performing this piece?

[i] BritshBattles.com says, “The Zulu warriors were formed in regiments by age, their standard equipment the shield and the stabbing spear. The formation for the attack, described as the “horns of the beast”, was said to have been devised by Shaka, the Zulu King who established Zulu hegemony in Southern Africa. The main body of the army delivered a frontal assault, called the “loins”, while the “horns” spread out behind each of the enemy’s flanks and delivered the secondary and often fatal attack in the enemy’s rear. Cetshwayo, the Zulu King, fearing British aggression took pains to purchase firearms wherever they could be bought. By the outbreak of war the Zulus had tens of thousands of muskets and rifles, but of a poor standard, and the Zulus were ill-trained in their use. The Zulus captured some 1,000 Martini Henry breech loading rifles and a large amount of ammunition. Some of these rifles were used at Rorke’s Drift. All the British casualties, few though they were, were shot rather than stabbed.

[ii] This is a posture dance performed by a group, with aggressive body movements and stamping of the feet with rhythmically shouted accompaniment and much eye bulging. War haka were originally performed by warriors before a battle, proclaiming their strength and prowess in order to intimidate the opposition and to fill the pants of the opposition.”

‘Ka mate Ka mate’ -It is death It is death

‘Ka ora Ka ora’ -It is life It is life

‘Ka mate Ka mate’

It is death It is death

Ka ora Ka ora -It is life It is life

Tenei Te Tangata Puhuruhuru-This is the hairy man

Nana i tiki mai whakawhiti te ra-Who caused the sun to shine again for me

Upane Upane-Up the ladder Up the ladder

Upane Kaupane-Up to the top

Whiti te ra-The sun shines!

| 47-66 | VOL 01 | MY MR. BIG BOJANGLES

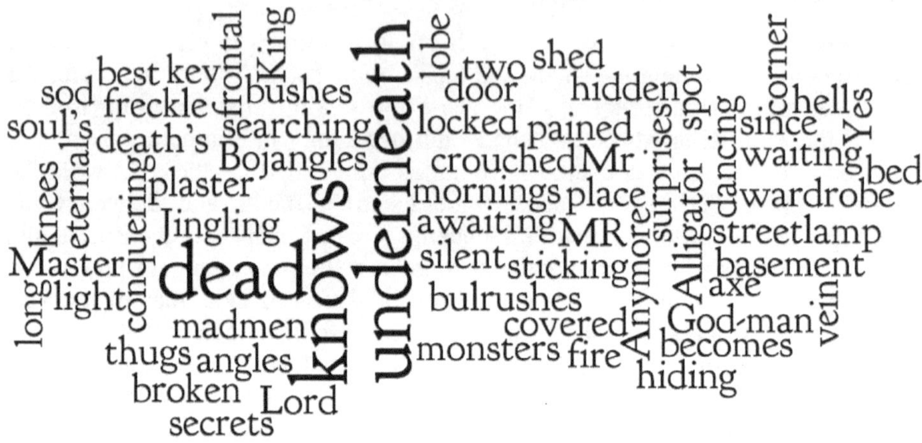

No secrets nor surprises for my King since dead

No monsters hidden underneath my bed

No madmen with an axe waiting in my wardrobe

No clotted vein in my headache pained and

Pounding frontal lobe

No locked door hiding who knows what

No freckle that becomes a cancer spot

No thugs around the corner crouched underneath

The broken streetlamp awaiting in the bushes

No, and

No silent Alligator in the long bulrushes

Of my mornings

Anymore

Yes, there is
No basement of the dead
He has not shed
His searching light upon
No place in the hell fire covered sod which
He has not trod
For this
Is
My conquering Lord and
My death's head [ii]dancing Master
My soul's scuffed knees eternal sticking plaster
The God-man who knows the best of all the angles
My two key Jingling
Mr. Big
Bojangles

-----O-----

PREAMBLE |

"I am He who lives, and was dead, and behold, I am alive forevermore. Amen. And I have the keys of Hades and of Death." (Revelation 1:18 NKJV)

EXPLANATION |

I was once again musing over dance. You see, I can't dance very well at all and it bothers me. It is Easter Sunday and I cannot get my favorite song to hate out of my head, you know, "Lord of the Dance."

I danced on a Friday when the world turned black
It's hard to dance with the devil on your back
They buried my body, they thought I was gone
But I am the dance, and the dance goes on

They cut me down and I leapt up high
I am the life that will never, never die
I'll live in you if you'll live in me
I am the Lord of the dance, said he

Even so, great lyrics! Terrible tune though, and presently in Blighty, quite an effeminate thought. I mean, he's probably just another dancing queen instead of a dancing King! I mean, I can't imagine a bunch of men singing this or prancing around. Unless they are part of the Officers Union in the Royal Navy. And we shall leave that statement right there!

Even so, King Jesus appears after His resurrection with two keys slung around his waist, and I don't know about you, but when I get new keys to a place, then I check it out most thoroughly. So then, there are no surprises for our God, nothing hidden nor nothing unexpected or unplanned for around our temporal or eternal corner. Nice. Oh, and by the way, I do think the Trinity dances. How about you? If resurrection Sunday does not make us dance, then how far we men have fallen from our all exuberant 'uber' joy.

PERFORMANCE TIPS |

With happiness and joy!

-----O-----

---

[i] I don't think there were any hidden beforehand either! Even so, there is, I think, a particular conquering and a particular asset counting and stripping, regarding the eternal takeover of both death and hell.

[ii] "Mr. Bojangles" is that 'legendery' sad song tale of a dancer in perpetual grief.

"I knew a man Bojangles and he'd dance for you
In worn out shoes, with silver hair, a ragged shirt, and baggy pants
The old soft shoe. He jumped so high, jumped so high
Then he lightly touched down

I met him in a cell in New Orleans I was down and out
He looked to me to be the eyes of age as he spoke right out
He talked of life, talked of life, he laughed clicked his heels and stepped

He said his name "Bojangles" and he danced a lick across the cell
He grabbed his pants and spread his stance,
Oh he jumped so high and then he clicked his heels
He let go a laugh, let go a laugh and shook back his clothes all around

Mr. Bojangles, Mr. Bojangles - Mr. Bojangles, dance

He danced for those at minstrel shows and county fairs throughout the south
He spoke through tears of 15 years how his dog and him traveled about
The dog up and died, he up and died and after 20 years he still grieves

He said I dance now at every chance in honky tonks for drinks and tips
But most the time I spend behind these county bars 'cause I drinks a bit
He shook his head, and as he shook his head I heard someone ask him please

Mr. Bojangles, Mr. Bojangles - Mr. Bojangles, dance."

| 48-66 | VOL 01 | CAN'T DANCE-WON'T DANCE!

[i]I can't dance
I am too self-aware
Rhythm is a dangerous thing
[ii]Ask a Catholic!
Just get out of synchronization once
And you pay for it the rest of your life

Syncopation
Syncopate
Sounds good
Until you try it
Getting elbows and knees
Feet, hips and chins
Eyes and lips

Neck and head
All to move in some kind of regular
Agreed fashion
To an external beat
Is beyond me
I see myself struggling in the mud
A fat bloke at the gym
Belly sucked in
Bum hanging out
There’s a lot of it about
You know?

It’s not that I can’t do it
It’s just that even when it’s OK, I look stupid!
Like a [iii]'Weeble' on speed
A stick insect wielding a shovel
[iv]John Major, drunk, chatting up Mrs. Thatcher
Nothing fits!
Know what I mean?

And I know it

Knowing it, introduces a tension to reluctant limbs
Resulting in minimalist movements

Now this is worse

Restricting an imbecile is always dangerous
But now I look like a Duracell Bunny gone bonkers

Nice people smile
Honest people spit out whatever they were drinking
Stop what they're thinking
Point and [v]guffaw
Clear the dance floor
And jive before me mockingly.

[vi]Can't dance.
Won't dance.

-----O-----

PREAMBLE |

Then David danced before the LORD with all his might; and David was wearing a linen ephod. So David and all the house of Israel brought up the ark of the LORD with shouting and with the sound of the trumpet. Now as the ark of the LORD came into the City of David, Michal, Saul's daughter, looked through a window and saw King David leaping and whirling before the LORD; and she despised him in her heart. (2 Sam 6:13-16 NKJV)

EXPLANATION |

You need three things to understand this poem. First, I can't dance. Second, I can't dance and third, I can't dance. My wife also despises my dancing. Nuff said.

PERFORMANCE TIPS |

With incredulity and many robot actions!

-----O-----

i This title, is based on a ridiculous Television Game show called 'Can't Cook, Won't Cook' Wikipedia says, "UK game show and cooking program that was broadcast on BBC 1 from 1995 to 1999. In it two people who either could not cook or would not cook were nominated to appear on the show the show by a friend or family member, the Host Chef would then set the two the task of cooking a certain meal. Once both participants had cooked these meals, the person who nominated them was blindfolded and sampled both versions of the meals; the winner was then the cook of the dish whom both blindfolded people nominated as the better tasting meal. In the case of a tie, the Host Chef would select the winner."

Like my dancing, the program was just awful!

ii Yes, I am referring to a method of conception control often used by old fashioned Roman Catholics back in the day! The rhythm method, also known as "fertility awareness," is a method of birth control that uses the menstrual cycle to predict your most fertile time of the month - that is when you are most likely to become pregnant. Once you have identified your most fertile time you simply don't make love during that time period. The large size of Roman Catholic families prove that either this method did not work, or in particular, that my own Scottish Roman Catholic roots were a most unrestrained group of folk!

iii The online vintage toy library says that "When Hasbro acquired Romper Room Inc. in 1969 the Weebles were on their way to Toy History. The Romper Room Show itself began in 1954 and was syndicated or franchised across America until the early seventies, when Weebles toys hit the marketplace. The genesis of these little toys that wobbled but never fell down was actually the Romper Room Punching Clown -- Weebles are tiny plastic versions of "bop-bags". So there you go!

'Speed' of course is a street name for Crystal Methamphetamine, the current drug that is decimating America that makes the user feel like superman and act twice as fast. When I dance, I do look like a 'Weeble on Speed!' How about that for a picture!

iv Mrs. Thatcher was the first woman Prime Minister in England. John Major, the grey man, was her successor. He did not really measure up and they did not really get on!

v Guffaw, a loud or boisterous burst of laughter

vi There is a serious side to this piece, honest. I suppose that there are always things that we feel we cannot do but know that we should do. If we are over the top in doing it or under par, the monstrous ridicule of others can stop up and further restrict us. In the end, such lack of affirmation can allow us to make a terminal declaration, which puts us in bondage for the rest of our lives. "Ï will never do that again! " Most Baptists have made this cultural declaration years ago, indeed it is a generational declaration! Their restrictive and judgmental nature about so many things essential to true liberty and religious freedom are testimony to this!

| 49-66 | VOL 01 | FOOT STOMPING CONTRITION

It is written

That a child must not be poked

You know, persistently

Provoked

To wrath.

Yet

Like an English student exiled in

Welsh speaking [i]Bangor

I am now

Engorged with rage, and

Furious in a foot stomping anger! For,

There has been no nurture, for me

Just a [ii]'bircher' with a bunch of branches

Flaying rhythmically over my

Poor
Praying
Back.
Though much admonition on Your rack
Oh yes
Much!
There's been nothing mild for this poor child
Just lots of tutting, and the
Shaking of stony fingers in my face, followed by
Slapped legs and a
Dunces hat with
Magnolia coated corner walls
For me to look and
Stare
Back
At

Through my bitter tears

It's
Just
Not
Fair!

And

It's not been fair for years.

It is written
That a child must not be poked
You know, persistently
Provoked
To wrath.
But I am like a tiger in a cage
Full of anger
Possessed by ripping rage
At You!

Is this any way for a faithful son to be treated?
Mistreated?
Tested weekly at my Lord's table
Burdened daily beyond that which I am able
To bear
Baited for so long that
I would become
The devil's own tongue of accusation toward Thee?

"You do not care for me! Yes,
By lack of provision with all this constant correction
Without any Seeming show of
Fatherly protection
You've treated me like a cuckoo and
Beat me like a red haired

Misfit
Love me? No,
You don't
Give a Shit!"

There.

I've said it."

And all Your mighty angels weep
And Satan says
"I'll [iii]succor you."

I think he has

A grown man should not be provoked
To cross his arms over his snotty
Grey and woolen 'jumpered' chest
To stick out his purple lip, and
Stomp around Your classroom in
His [iv]'Wellies'
This is the marching of a child.
Selfish.
Unseeing.
Foolish.
Little.

Father, please treat my tantrum as
You would treat a child
For such accusation from the mouth of a man
Deserves,
Discipline
Deserves,
Years in the can
So,
If
You
Can
No,
If You will
Spare Your wrath and do not kill
For now, O Lord
I beg You,
Please
Be my Savior, yes and O my God be mild,
Forgive my pissy, petty petulance, and come and
Treat me like a little child.

-----O-----

PREAMBLE |

And, ye fathers, provoke not your children to wrath: but bring them up in the nurture and admonition of the Lord. (Ephesians 6:4 KJV)

...and that you put on the new man which was created according to God, in true righteousness and holiness. (Ephesians 4:24 NKJV)

...and have put on the new man who is renewed in knowledge according to the image of Him who created him, (Colossians 3:10 NKJV)

EXPLANATION |

There are times I must be treated like a child. Else I be mightily disciplined, even killed. The older I get, the less I seem to understand the ways of the Lord with a man. The older I get, the less I understand David and the more I seem to know Saul. This is not good. Though, I am learning that bent knees, do not lead to bended hearts, and oh yes, there is a difference between a bent heart and a bended one. Do you know what I mean?

The new man, if we have him, will always call for a bending, a bowing, an always defending of the constancy of God in His own unbending love toward me. Do you have the new man? Do you hear him speak, even in your flying anger?

Remember, the truth is, that many Christians will go through a season of feeling like this. There is no real answer for such seasons except faith and hope. And where the line of accusation has been crossed, and boy do we cross it sometimes, the sooner we get to the place of contrition, the safer we will be.

As for me, there are times I must be treated like a child. Else I be mightily disciplined, even killed.

PERFORMANCE TIPS |

Be petulant! Be full of self-pity, emphasize the words, 'my' and 'poor', and be as self-indulgent as you can without getting too 'hammy'.

Make 'Stare, back, at,' sound like the slapping of the back of legs if you can.

When it comes to 'it's just not fair!' Stomp your foot to each individual word like a child wearing wellingtons.

Before you move on to confession, you know, 'There' I've said it..' make sure that there is a shocked silence after the strong accusation, whose three words should be said and sounded as a single word with three syllables.

After the same two words, 'Deserves', I think the comma should be annunciated with a seen reflective pause before pronouncing the judicial sentence of the next line.

-----O-----

---

[i] In 2011 I went to Bangor when I toured the then 66 Cities of the UK speaking from each of the 66 Books of The Bible in just 66 Days. I tried to speak at the BBC, but being a non-welsh speaker I could not even get into reception! Bangor, is the beating heart of 'Plaid Cymru' the Welsh Nationalist Party. Though the university may be great, I wonder if the English are suffered in Bangor. I tell, on that particular day, I was not best pleased!

[ii] In the middle of the Irish Sea, the Isle of Man, with a population of about 50,000, is a Crown Dependency. It is not part of the UK and has its own parliament and makes its own laws. These are often similar to British laws, but the island did not follow the mainland in abolishing judicial corporal punishment in 1948. It still 'Birches' people today. A birch rod is not a single rod of wood and also not necessarily made from birch twigs, indeed, a hazel rod is particularly painful when applied across the bared buttocks. Ouch! A bundle of four or five hazel twigs was used in the 1960's and 1970's on the Isle of Man and though birching is still law there, it's not been practiced for a while.

[iii] As in 'sucker'!

[iv] Wellingtons. As a stomping child, I found that 'Wellies' made a much louder noise when the rubber slapped against may calves as I stomped.

| 50-66 | VOL 01 | CANDY CRUSH SAGA

You're a cool drink that needs sipping

You're a flower that needs picking

You're a carrot that needs dipping

In the guacamole of my heart

You're a sausage that needs pricking

You're an ice cream that needs licking

You're a keepsake that needs sticking

'Tween' my sheets

You're a duvet that needs wrapping

Round my shoulders on a dark and stormy night

You're a tower to [i]retreat to in my fright

You're a freesia's sweet perfume
The soft shade that lifts my gloom
You're the silver edgéd moon

That lights my night!

You're a [ii]table spread before me
in the presence of my foes
You're a bowl of steaming pasta
That can soak up all my woes
Yes, you're the curl in all my toes

You know you are

You are hot and alcoholic,
You're the spring that makes me frolic
You're the fondue where I'll dip my mouth's delight
Oh! You are food and drink to me
Yes you're just my cup of tea
You're the pleasing shape
That strokes my peering sight

Tonight!

-----*O*-----

PREAMBLE |

Behold, you are fair, my love! Behold, you are fair! You have dove's eyes behind your veil. Your hair is like a flock of goats, Going down from Mount Gilead. 2 Your teeth are like a flock of shorn sheep Which have come up from the washing, Every one of which bears twins, And none is barren among them. 3 Your lips are like a strand of scarlet, And your mouth is lovely. Your temples behind your veil Are like a piece of pomegranate. 4 Your neck is like the tower of David ,Built for an armory, On which hang a thousand bucklers, All shields of mighty men. 5 Your two breasts are like two fawns, Twins of a gazelle, Which feed among the lilies.6 Until the day breaks And the shadows flee away, I will go my way to the mountain of myrrh And to the hill of frankincense. (Song 4:1-6 NKJV)

EXPLANATION |

This is a poem of promise, indeed, if you are [iii] 'on a promise' it's great one to recite to your beloved..

PERFORMANCE TIPS |

Have fun The separate one liners need saying with some pointed definiteness and preferably playfully and publicly with your beloved. Embarrass her.

-----O-----

---

i

I will love You, O Lord, my strength.
The Lord is my rock and my fortress and my deliverer;
My God, my strength, in whom I will trust;
My shield and the horn of my salvation, my stronghold.
I will call upon the Lord, who is worthy to be praised;
So shall I be saved from my enemies.
(Ps 18:1-3NKJV)

The name of the Lord is a strong tower;
The righteous run to it and are safe.
(Prov 18:10 NKJV)

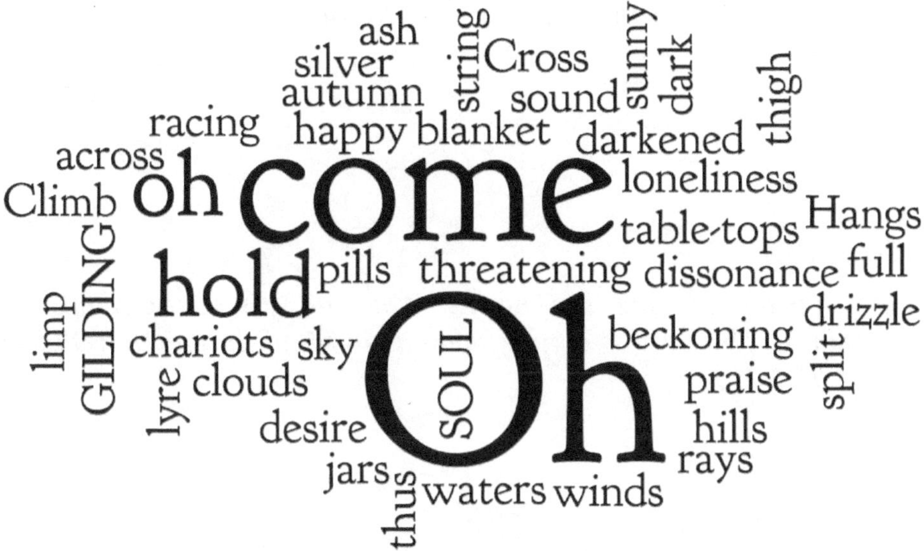

When thus the darkened waters

Climb the threatening hills

When table-tops are full of ash

And jars of beckoning pills

When dissonance is the only sound

On the dark string of my lyre

Oh come to me, oh come to me

Oh hold me, my desire

When silver chariots of happy clouds

Cross the racing sky

When the blanket of my loneliness

Hangs limp across my thigh

When the autumn winds and drizzle

Are split by sunny rays
Oh come to me, oh come to me
Oh hold me, Oh my praise

-----O-----

PREAMBLE |

The chariots of God are twenty thousand, Even thousands of thousands; The Lord is among them as in Sinai, in the Holy Place. (Ps 68:17 KJV)

EXPLANATION |

A simple prayer of desperate desire.

PERFORMANCE TIPS |

Weep it.

-----O-----

---

ii The Lord is my shepherd; I shall not want. He makes me to lie down in green pastures; He leads me beside the still waters. He restores my soul; He leads me in the paths of righteousness For His name's sake.

Yea, though I walk through the valley of the shadow of death, I will fear no evil; For You are with me; Your rod and Your staff, they comfort me.

You prepare a table before me in the presence of my enemies; You anoint my head with oil; My cup runs over. 6 Surely goodness and mercy shall follow me All the days of my life; And I will dwell in the house of the Lord Forever.

(Ps 23 NKJV)

iii 'on a promise' means to be confidently assured of something, especially of having sexual intercourse, or of making luuuuuuuurrrv.

| 52-66 | VOL 01 | ABOMINATION

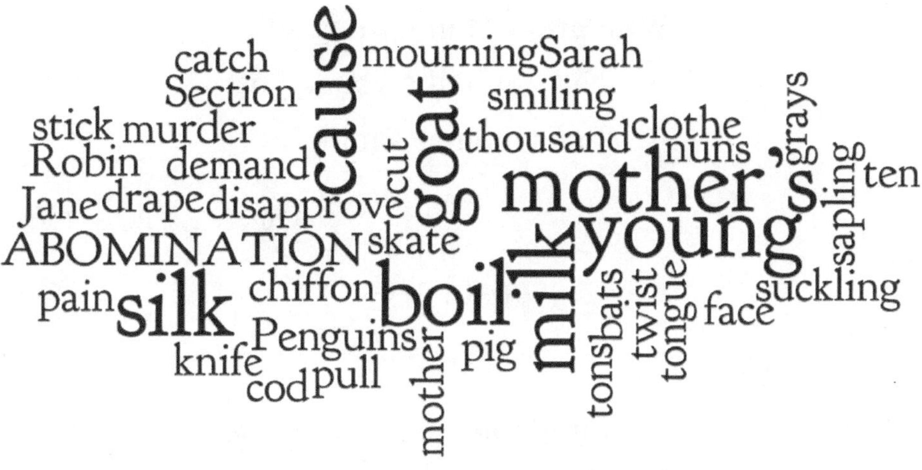

You shall not boil a young goat
In its mother's milk
You shall not clothe a suckling pig
With chiffon or with silk
You shall not disapprove
[i]Of Section 28
You shall not catch a cod, and
Demand that he should skate
You shall not cause a Robin
To pull ten thousand tons
You shall not stick your tongue out
At Penguins, bats or nuns
You shall not twist a knife
Or cause a mother pain

You shall not cut a sapling
Nor murder Sarah Jane
You shall not drape a smiling face
With grays of mourning silk
You shall not boil a young goat
In its mother's milk

-----O-----

PREAMBLE |

The first of the first fruits of your land you shall bring to the house of the LORD your God. You shall not boil a young goat in its mother's milk." Ex 34:26

EXPLANATION |

I came across the first two lines of this poem, when I was preaching my way through Exodus. It laid hold of me. Frankly I didn't understand it, but then, on that same evening, the news presented me with a pleading mother, whose daughter was later found murdered, pleaded with her unknown abductor for her safe return, and she did so, through red eyes, set on puffed cheeks, underscored with dark shadows, all simmering with grief. And then I knew.

PERFORMANCE TIPS |

With great sadness.

-----O-----

---

[i] The Telegraph reported in November 2015 that David Cameron says "sorry" over Section 28 gay law. "David Cameron has publicly apologised for Section 28 the law introduced by the Thatcher government banning local authorities from promoting homosexuality. The Tory leader, speaking at a Gay pride event, went much further than before in apologising for decisions taken by the party when Baroness Thatcher was leader. Mr Cameron, the first Tory leader to speak at a Gay pride event, said: "I am sorry for Section 28. We got it wrong. It was an

emotional issue. I hope you can forgive us." Section 28, which became law in 1988, banned local authorities from portraying homosexuality in a positive light. It became a totemic issue for Conservative modernisers. In 2003, when it was abolished by the Labour government, Mr Cameron voted for only the partial lifting of the ban."

Mr Cameron is a vote catching idiot, and I say that with all the respect I can muster. However, this poem is not about Sodomy.

The furnace orange moon
Hung scimitar like over
The black prostrate sea.

I hope for your love like a
Crazy man would shoot
Arrows At the moon.

My night clouds are lit
With edg-ed silver, as your
Blue light fills my sky.

My cheeks leave your kiss
To swoon from the tranquil sea

Of your silver moon.

-----O-----

PREAMBLE |

Praise Him, sun and moon; Praise Him, all you stars of light! (Psalm 148:3)

EXPLANATION |

Haiku is a poetic form and a type of poetry from Japanese culture. Haiku combines form, content and language in a meaningful, yet compact form. The most common form for Haiku is three short lines. The first line usually contains five syllables, the second line seven syllables, and the third line contains five syllables. Haiku doesn't rhyme and must paint a mental image in the reader's mind. To put the poem's meaning and imagery in the reader's mind in just seventeen syllables over just three lines of poetry can be somewhat of a challenge Concerning haikus, well, I am still tying my shoes.

PERFORMANCE TIPS |

I don't think these are for performance!

-----O-----

| 54-66 | VOL 01 | THE PRODIGALS PLIGHT

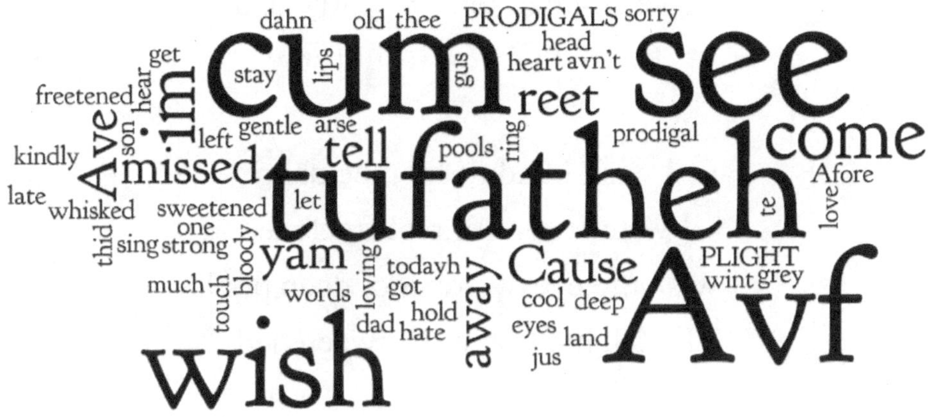

Avf cum tu see me fatheh
Is jus cum in todayh
I wint te see im at is arse
But thid whisked him reet away

Avf cum tu see me fatheh
Cause we avn't spoken much
An I've missed is kindly words
Ave missed is gentle touch

Avf cum tu see me fatheh
Cause I've only got but one
And I yam is bloody prodigal
And I yam is loving son

Avf cum tu see me fatheh
Afore he gus away
I've come to tell im "sorry dad
I wish that you would stay

I wish I hadn't let thee dahn
I wish I weren't reet freetened
I wish me eyes were cool deep pools
I wish me lips were sweetened

Avf cum tu see me fatheh
Before it's all too late
To tell 'im that I love him
That I've left the land of hate

Avf cum tu see me fatheh
Ave come to get me ring
I've come to hold his old grey head
And hear his strong heart sing

-----O-----

PREAMBLE |

I will arise and go to my father, and will say to him, "Father, I have sinned against heaven and before you, and I am no longer worthy to be called your son. Make me like one of your hired servants." (Luke 15:17-19 NKJV)

EXPLANATION |

We'd raced up the M1, my wife a consumed passenger, praying that she would get to her mum's bedside before she died. Whilst she ran , I wandered into the reception of the county hospital, when someone else in a desperate hurry and with the broadest of 'Derbyshire accents,' requested to see his father. Obviously he had some urgent heart business to attend do. Many of us, still have. This poem is my son's most favourite poem.

PERFORMANCE TIPS |

This poem is to be read in a rush and with the broadest of Derbyshire accents!

-----O-----

| 55-66 | VOL 01 | THE SCARLET FLOWER

I am a jaunty Cavalier
Of soft soap and of flannel
Delivering thankful 'Frenchies'
Across the English Channel

I am a smart purveyor
Of all things bright and clean
Stealing bent bared necks
From Madam Guillotine

I am a high aristocrat
I am a Poncey Percy
Bursting into dungeon cells
And showing sinners mercy

I am the Scarlet Pimpernel
In the face of revolution
Snatching timid tearful souls
From the jaws of dissolution

I am the one from which you hide
I'm the one whom you do seek
I am the one you worship
On the seventh day of the week

I am the loving saving God
I am the great last bleeder
I am the Savior of the tart
I'll clothe and love and feed her

I am the scarlet flower
Hung between cross beams
I am the God of judgment
I am the God of means

Means to save and means to send
Means to have a party
Means to gather in all men
Even Russell Harty

For, I am The Scarlet Pimpernel

In the face of revolution
Snatching timid tearful souls
From the jaws of dissolution

-----O-----

PREAMBLE |

But I am a worm, and no man; A reproach of men, and despised of the people. All those who see Me ridicule Me; They shoot out the lip, they shake the head, saying, "He trusted in the LORD, let Him rescue Him; Let Him deliver Him, since He delights in Him! (Ps 22:6-8 NKJV)

EXPLANATION |

Wikipedia says that "The Scarlet Pimpernel is a classic play and adventure novel by Baroness Emmuska Orczy, set during the French Revolution. It was first produced as a record-breaking play in an adaptation by Julia Neilson and Fred Terry..... Marguerite Blakeney, a beautiful French actress, is married to wealthy English fop, Sir Percy Blakeney. The couple has become estranged due to her earlier unintentional denunciation of French aristocrat the Marquis de St. Cyr and his family, which resulted in their being sent to the guillotine. Like many others, Marguerite is entranced by stories of the Scarlet Pimpernel — an anonymous hero who, through a combination of courage and daring, has rescued many aristocrats from Madame la Guillotine, and brought them safely to England." Of course it is the fop himself, Sir Percey Blakeney who is in fact the Scarlet Pimpernel. Baroness Emmuska will fall in love with this great redeemer and find him to be her husband.

PERFORMANCE TIPS |

If you can put on a foppish English accent, then do so for the reading of this poem. (I beg my American friends not even to try this...it's far too painful for the rest of us. We still haven't forgiven you for Mary

Poppins and Dick Van Dyke's utter slaughter of the Cockney dialect. No, please don't even try!)

Change your accent at the line, "Snatching timid tearful souls" where Jesus now begins to speak...OK, fops away!

-----O-----

Herbert had a wife, and
His wifey's name was Jael, and
Jael, she had a panache
With a hammer and a nail

For with a hammer and a nail
She fixed him to the spot
With a hammer and a stake
She put a hole right through the snake

Now
Adam had a wife
His wifey's name was Eve, and
Eve she had a problem

That helped them both to leave, but

With a hammer and a nail
She fixed him to the spot
With a hammer and a stake
She put a hole right through the snake

Now
Lizzy had a cousin
That cousin's name was Mary, and
Mary was a gentle girl and
Not at all
Contrary, yet

With a hammer and a nail
She fixed him to the spot
With a hammer and a stake
She put a hole right through the snake

Now
The Father had a Son and
That lovely Son was
Jesus
He hung wrapped round a bronzéd pole
To die and save and keep us, for

With a hammer and a nail

He was fixed right to the spot
With a hammer and a stake
He put a hole right through the
Sssssssssnake!

-----O-----

PREAMBLE |

Stand still and consider the wondrous works of God. (Num 21:8)

Then the LORD said to Moses, "Make a fiery serpent, and set it on a pole; and it shall be that everyone who is bitten, when he looks at it, shall live." (Job 37:14 NKJV)

And the LORD has laid on Him the iniquity of us all. (Isa 53:6 NKJV)

EXPLANATION |

There is no subtext here. Jael, what a gal! What a blow! What a truth! Have a look at Judges 4:17 onwards. Oh by the way, I know she was married to Heber the Kenite, and not Herbert the Kenite but maybe Herbert would be a modern translation of his ancient name? Maybe!

PERFORMANCE TIPS |

This poem is to be read with gusto! It has a constant foot tapping tempo and needs an awful lot of breath. So, breathe deeply! The words 'nail' and 'stake' are good points to take a deep, deep breath!

-----O-----

| 57-66 | VOL 01 | LOW PAVEMENTS

The witness of wealth in brown and dappled marble stone
Is reflected on ice blue cold floor
Where his souls now stand alone
Exhausted by men's hate
Panting and bowed already
With the black gown of men's grief
Mauve and marred
He has become almost featureless,
Beyond the tan of men
Mauled by red handed machines
Mocked without sympathy
From grey lips dulled to death
In death dripped red
On ripped dripped blood spattered

Pavement floor
Dusted in the rust of autumn fading
That tastes of iron within his mouth
That will soon split tender tendons
That once so lovingly caressed
The fallen and forgotten
Now hiding in the long shadows of a
Darkened sun
Bathed in a green sea of envy
That glitters with the blurting red of a rising jealousy
From those who once adored and walked in gold
Amongst the shining stones on the Northern slopes
Of heavens King of Ages
To the bubbling Sulphur yellow of the lake prepared

The mob cried, "Crucify!"
And "Crucify!" again

Until the Son is lifted high
In the colors of Gabbatha.

-----O-----

PREAMBLE |

Then Jesus came out, wearing the crown of thorns and the purple robe. And Pilate said to them, "Behold the Man!" (John 19:5 NKJV)

EXPLANATION |

Gabbatha, is the Hebrew word for the place where Jesus stood alone, before the judgment seat of Pilate. (John 19:13) .This poem is another pale attempt once more, to describe a portion of His indescribable 'Passion', in word colors.

PERFORMANCE TIPS |

With tears.

-----O-----

| 58-66 | VOL 01 | DEATH'S DESPISING OF BEAUTY WASTED

The wakeful termite would titillate the
Bedridden and vulgar pilgrim
Who sorely squirmed on soft sores
Who, aging quickly like a slobbering vegetable
Puts out his false teeth
In deaths rancid and poisoned waters.
Plink,
Plink,
Glup!

The tortured corpse looks up and forces a gummy smile, and
Gasps out the sickening breath that
Runs in rancorous rasps along the tortured tepid tongue

Decked in dry black cancer
To greet the smiling termite.

Soon it would be dinner time.

Outside, in the rain
The rogue patrol
With defiant scissors had cut the respectable silence
Leaving the jagged edges hanging lazily in burnt out bins
Of blackened red
In green parks
Peppered with scattered cushioned tarmac
Whilst the sultana-nosed dog sniffed
The stiff ballerina, and
Cocked his leg once more.

-----O-----

PREAMBLE |

His strength is starved, And destruction is ready at his side. It devours patches of his skin; The firstborn of death devours his limbs. He is uprooted from the shelter of his tent, And they parade him before the king of terrors (Job 18:12-14 NKJV)

EXPLANATION |

In ignorance we think we shall smile at death, and in reality, a few do. My mother, riddled with cancer, coughed her smoked up lungs upon my bed as she brought me tea each morning. In her last few days on the last bed at the departure end of the ward, along with her hallucinations and visitations from our old dead dog, already ghost-

like, she gripped the sides of the bed, (fearful that if she did not then she would float up to the ceiling) as her dentures in the dirty lukewarm glass smiled at me. I noticed a dry black scab in the center of her tongue. The cancer was eating her alive.

PERFORMANCE TIPS |

This is a poem of pointlessness. The old die horribly, the younger generation think they are defiant against the inevitable and that they can change things for good, forever, at least for themselves.

Their statement of beautiful defiance twirls like a stiff pop-up plastic ballerina on an old music box, whilst the Heinz 57 dog of fate pisses nonchalantly on its twirling cogs. If you can capture that picture in the mood, I think you shall communicate well!

| 59-66 | VOL 01 | LIVING VOICES

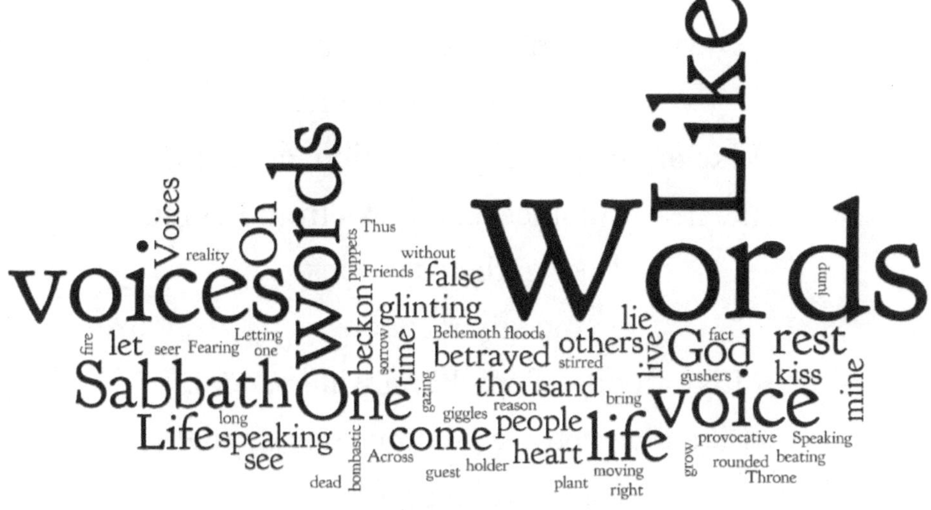

Above technology I begin to see
Words that beckon, beckon me
Single statement of simplicity
Come hear, come know, come see, come grow

And there they stand
Voluminous, secret, pregnant, provocative,
Beautiful, curved, hard words

Words that wobble, words that leer,
Words of the prophet and of the seer
Words that hit and words that miss
Words that spit and words that kiss
Words for the young

Words for the older
Words that shield the quaking holder

For behind the Words
Like shields and swords
Like armor glinting, growling, creaking
Like heavy clothes and ducks from Peking
Like garlands moons
And silver spoons
Like floods of sparkling waters, cool,
Like love betrayed, betrayed and cruel
Like frothing gushers
From rounded mounds,
Like glinting giggles
From painted clowns

Hides the animators

Even a thousand voices

For words are mere puppets of the voice
Words are ventriloquist's dummies
Made to jump by the moving heart

And one is mine
One heart beating
One voice speaking

One time
On a Tuesday, hanging out the washing
Speaking through a mouth gripping wooden pegs
Holding onto life's line,
Hanging out my wet and dripping hopes to dry
Looking at the sky!
Blinking, gazing at the blue and whites of wisps
On cold cheeks dead
Red with sorrow, blushing with hope
Of a better tomorrow,
Oh let the warmth plant a tender kiss
Oh let there be more, oh more than this
More than this
Oh, more than this,

If voices were out, and speaking,
Then we could expect a revolution
For voices when freed
Are voices that that will unite
And voices that will call
For an end to it all
To bring a burning beginning of bouncing boisterousness
To Badges beavering and burrowing beneath
The blunt bellows of bombastic emptiness
Emerging to behold

Behemoth!

Painting him with right words once more
Leading leviathan with a hook
Loving him
Letting him play with small maidens
While merchants make a banquet for the long guest
Lest he be stirred, and
Sneeze fire
Across their wilderness, but

Voices sin, and
Voices hide, and
Crouch like dogs
Beaten
Fearing to lift themselves
To the sterner faces
Of false realities, and

How can a reality be false?

Well, when it is in fact a lie
Dressed up in bitterness, and forgetfulness, and reason
Thus dressed
Reality is a lie!

When it has no rhythm, has no rhyme,

Splits the whole with schism of soul, and
Robs a man of Sabbath time.
Sabbath rest, Sabbath mine

For there is a rest for the people of God, and
What are true poets, but
The people of God at rest

Sabbath voices on a carrier wave of a thousand others
With frequency of but One
The Masters voice

All others are but observers of the helix of life

For there is life in a voice
Life in the thunder
Life in the lightening
Life in the whispering from The Throne
Of Him who is life of life and
God alone

Friends, you cannot live without a voice, and

Only voices shall live!

-----O-----

PREAMBLE |

And from the throne proceeded lightnings, thunderings, and voices…….. (Rev 4:4 NKJV)

EXPLANATION |

I love words and the sound they make. I love words and the pictures they paint. I love words, especially the way they move my lips and touch my heart. This poem is about the magic and wonder of words. You will also notice that I love alliteration! I leave the same consonant lying around so much that you might just fall over it, so be careful now.

I love reading the book of Job. The oldest book in the Bible, is jam-packed full of poetry and possible dinosaurs as well. No honest! Have a look at chapters 40 & 41. Some versions of the Bible attempt to make these awesome words more accessible, by inserting what they believe to be the nearest thing we know and are all familiar with, just to make us feel safe. But really, how on earth could the descriptions of Leviathan and Behemoth, be adequately translated into 'Crocodile' and 'Hippopotamus'! It's just ridiculous. By this substitution, already the names have lost some secret majesty they once possessed. Leave them as they are, for as they are, they possess a voice. Let's leave it like that shall we? Voices are important.

Probably the most important things we possess. Indeed if I were ever to place my views on poetic expression as a philosophy of life it would be that God created voices and voices released bring revolution and true liberty. This poem IS my philosophy for life..

PERFORMANCE TIPS |

Be a mad scientist, begin with glasses and then take them off and speak wide eyed when you start hanging out the washing!

| 60-66 | VOL 01 | WHO THE HECK ARE YOU!

Who the heck am I?
Well who the heck are you?
What do you do?

Where you from
Are you Da bomb
Baby?
Where you are from
Maybe?

Who the heck are you?

Who the heck am I?
Did I fly

In today in some plush pushy
Fine, arrive on time
Private jet
That yet
Has to be paid for
By my forthcoming record sales
And tales
Of the
Unexpected
Tax inspected
Fuel injected
SUV
You see
Yes you
See
Well you think you do
You know?

See

ME!

But you don't
Oh no, just this
This tattooed tailored
Shell
This silicon implanted

No I won't tell, baby!
I won't tell baby!
I won't yell baby!
At the tampered tempered
Badly invented
[i]Botox piece enhancer

[ii]Do you want your peace enhancing?
Bet you do
Bet you do
You know?
Want your peace enhancing
Bet you will, bet you do
Yeah, who the heck am I?
Well who the heck are you!

Who Am I?
Did I walk in today
Do I walk the talk, today
Tell tall tales today
That unclothe secret sighs
Greased thighs
French fries, minced pies, blue skies,
Black-eyed lies
Hiding
Secret nakedness

Waiting
Pleading, bleeding, leading me
In a verbal dance of the seven veils
To Peal back and
Disrobe the darkness
Unclothe the truth about me
The truth about you
Newanda,
Shanda,
Toshiba
Honda,
Jake and Ike,
Sue and Mike,
The truth is there, there in the night
Like a sharp spike
In the center of your pillow
Where you lay your head
Your dead head
Drowning in
Warped visioned
Cat-ar-actic night sight
Where you might

You might

Well, you know

You might

Dream truths, and then
Call them nightmares, and then
Deny 'em
Fry 'em
Justify 'em

But baby!!!!
The truth goes on

On and up
Up the apples
Up the apples
[iii]Up the apples and the pears
Where your dreams
Steam you through the night
Right

Right to the truth

Yeah right
Yeah right to truth

Yeah maybe baby
Yeah maybe

The truth will get ya!

Oh Baby will
Oh Baby do
Tell me sweetie
Tell me do

Who the heck am I ? And

Who the heck are you?

-----O-----

PREAMBLE |

"Not everyone who says to Me, 'Lord, Lord,' shall enter the kingdom of heaven, but he who does the will of My Father in heaven. Many will say to Me in that day, 'Lord, Lord, have we not prophesied in Your name, cast out demons in Your name, and done many wonders in Your name?' And then I will declare to them, 'I never knew you ; depart from Me, you who practice lawlessness! (Matt 7:21-23 NKJV)

EXPLANATION |

This is very much a shock and awe introductory piece. It is best performed whilst wandering around the folks seated at tables and preferably just inches from several select faces! It is best to prime these people beforehand, especially if they are big, muscular and hairy! It's great fun and is a brilliant ease into then introducing yourself in fuller terms as a poet. Yes there is reference to male herbal enhancements products. 'Smiling Bob' tells me that over ten million have been sold!

Oh and finally, for my American friends, an introduction to some Victorian Pig Latin or what's better known as Cockney Rhyming Slang is in the Notes. Enjoy!

PERFORMANCE TIPS |

Go get in someone's face and be very bonkers when performing this. The double entendre's are obvious, make them so. !

-----O-----

---

[i] There has to be something wacky about a society that injects Botulism, a form of food poisoning into the facial area to get rid of wrinkles! When people die from Botulism it is often because it has gotten into their chest and paralyzed their respiratory muscles so they cannot breathe! In the same way, the injections paralyze face muscles to stop the frowning muscle contractions! People who do this often look more peaceful, you know, like a corpse laid out for viewing!

ii Now remember this is performance poetry! It is an art form and here is a chance for some fun. When you perform this section, be sure to be in the face of the biggest guy there and then stare into his crotch as you say the words. This of course is a direct reference to 'Enzyte', (the penis pill) the erectile dysfunction pill used by Smiling Bob. Enzyte claims their product will improve male sexual function and performance and give them firmer, fuller-feeling erections. Again this is comment on fallen society that insists real women need to have large breasts even if it means silicone implants and real men, well real men need their own golf club! What a pitiful and pathetic ridiculous state affairs we have gotten ourselves into when the size bodily appendages is the true measure of a person's vitality attractiveness and worth. God help us!

iii The webs 'Greatest Dick'n' Arry of Cockney Rhyming Slang' (it isn't by the way!) says that "Cockney rhyming slang is not a language but a collection of phrases used by Cockneys and other Londoners. A true Cockney is someone born within the sound of Bow Bells. (St Mary-le-Bow Church in Cheapside, London).However the term Cockney is now loosely applied to many born outside this area as long as they have a "Cockney" accent or a Cockney heritage.The Cockney accent is heard less often in Central London these days but is widely heard in the outer London boroughs, the London suburbs and all across South East England. It is common in Bedfordshire towns like Luton and Leighton Buzzard, and Essex towns such as Romford.Rhyming Slang phrases are derived from taking an expression which rhymes with a word and then using that expression instead of the word. For example the word "look" rhymes with "butcher's hook". In many cases the rhyming word is omitted - so you won't find too many Londoners having a "bucher's hook" at this site, (http://www.cockneyrhymingslang.co.uk/cockney_rhyming_slang) but you might find a few having a "butcher's". The rhyming word is not always omitted so Cockney expressions can vary in their construction, and it is simply a matter of convention which version is used.

Here are some Cockney rhyming slang for parts of the body

English Cockney Rhymes:

Feet	=Plates of meat	= Plates
Teeth	=Hampstead Heath	=Hampsteads
Legs	=Scotch eggs	=Scotches
Eyes	=Mince pies	=Minces
Hair	=Barnet Fair	=Barnet
Head	=Loaf of bread	=Loaf

And of Course

Apples and Pears are a housing reference. Have you got it yet?

Apples and Pairs = Stairs!

| 61-66 | VOL 01 | MODELLING MODESTY

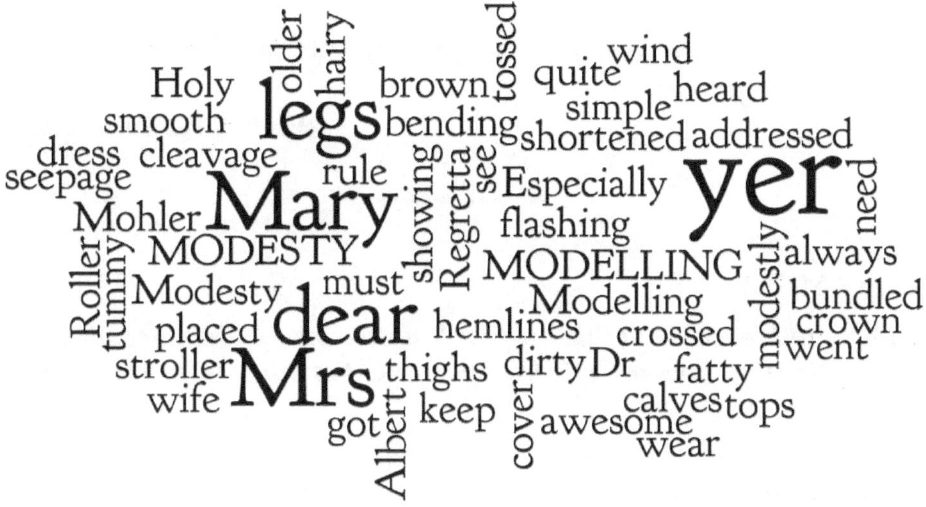

I heard of 'Modelling Modesty' by Mrs. Mary Mohler
The wife of Dr. Albert, that awesome Holy Roller
So I bundled up Regretta and placed her in her stroller
And went to see what hemlines I should wear as I got older

"You must cover up your legs my dear"
I was addressed by Mrs. Mary
"Especially smooth brown thighs
And calves that are quite hairy
There is no need for shortened tops
And fatty tummy seepage
Or bending down, showing yer crown
And flashing all yer cleavage.

No, the simple rule for you my dear
The dirty and the wind tossed
Is that you dress most modestly
And always keep yer legs crossed!"

-----O-----

PREAMBLE |

But go and learn what this means: 'I desire mercy and not sacrifice.' For I did not come to call the righteous, but sinners, to repentance (Matt 9:13 NKJV)

EXPLANATION |

Modelling Modesty – Or- Practical Advice For The Teenage Mother of African American Regretta Daze.

I was at Southern Seminary where I saw a sign for ladies where the wife of the president (The Awesome Dr Albert Mohler) was giving a talk to ladies on fashion called "Modelling Modesty!" This poem is to be read from the point of view of a teenage African America single mother, who passing the seminary on her way to 'Walgreans' saw the same add and attended the presentation! No criticism toward Dr Al or Mrs. Mary is intended whatsoever!

PS. My wife was also the Director of a Crisis Pregnancy centre in Redneck Central Kentucky (I love Kentucky!) and this problem of teenage pregnancy is by no means an African American one, except for Rednecks, it seemed to be planned teenage pregnancy! Anyways, before I get myself into anymore hot water than I already am in, I shall shut up.

PERFORMANCE TIPS |

With fun and a naughty glint in your eye. !

-----O-----

| 62-66 | VOL 01 | DIARRHEATRIBE

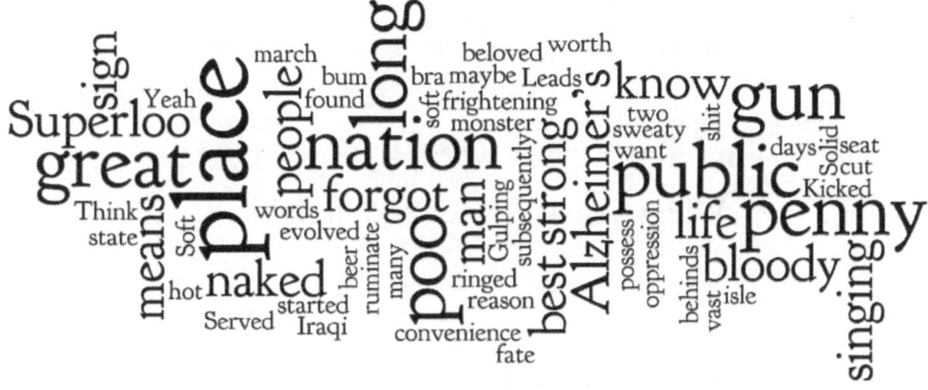

I want to spend a penny

I need a [i]number two

Do you know what I am intimating

Does it mean a thing to you?

'Cause in my great beloved nation

In that soft and sceptered isle,

A penny means relief you know

Yes, a penny now means style!

For we've evolved from Mr. [ii]Crappers

Outdated way to poo,

To the shiny singing

Soft and gleaming

Solid silver

[iii]Superloo.

Surely, it's a certain sign of
Pearly prized progression, and
To those who don't possess it
Well, it's sign of strong oppression

[iv]For tell me, what worth a strong republic
When a man cannot poo in public?

Yeah, you can shoot or go fur trappin'
But still strain to keep the crap in, and
In a nation full of people of
Every shape and kind
Is this the frightening reason
There are so many vast behinds?

For what is a man to do,
When in public he cannot poo?

The lack of this proud convenience
Leads to 'bowely' disobedience
For where there is no place to remonstrate,
No public place to ruminate,
Lies a local vocal vacuum, and
The fate of the
Late great nation state

Served on a plate,
Mate,
To a gun toting voting people, doting
On the safety that money and technology
Evidently is bringing singing
Into safe cities ringed around
The vortex of the
Cerebral cortex,
Kicked high
By the thigh-slapping monster
Still heading west
Though this time naked and
Without a cotton vest
But what's best
For me
What's best
for you,

A car and a gun

But no Superloo!

On reflection,
It is evident
That [v]Abram had no tank
Just sweaty armpits that stank

At the end of his long march home.

On hot days he gazed
Into the shimmering distance
Longing for a city that was not here
That, and a [vi]donkey, and maybe
A long, cold,
Budweiser beer.
He had no place to lay his head
No seat to place his bum, and
Today, [vii]Moses he has Alzheimer's
Alzheimer's and a gun!
Think about it.

America is not quite well.
Her enormous boat is sinking.
She should have woken up
Woken up and started
Thinking,
Drinking ,
Gulping in the words of life
Instead of begin to cut her wrists along
A long Iraqi knife. and

Bleed out her bloody, bloody life.

Whilst playing the goat and

Not the hare
She forgot her shirt and bra,
She forgot her underwear, and

Subsequently, was found naked
Shivering in her shit
Shot up once again, and
Shot down.
Down,
Down,
Goes the
Melted clown.
Shoeless,
Clueless,
In a great big land
That is,

Superloo-Less.

-----O-----

PREAMBLE |

Then Eliakim the son of Hilkiah, Shebna, and Joah said to the Rabshakeh, "Please speak to your servants in Aramaic, for we understand it; and do not speak to us in Hebrew in the hearing of the people who are on the wall." But the Rabshakeh said to them, "Has my master sent me to your master and to you to speak these

words, and not to the men who sit on the wall, who will eat and drink their own waste with you?" (2 Kings 18:26,27 NKJV)

EXPLANATION |

Webster describes a diatribe as prolonged discourse, a bitter and abusive speech or writing containing ironic or satirical criticism. Well here is a 'Diarrheatribe' and yes, this poem is full of it! This is not a political poem. This is not a comment on a Labour, Conservative, Liberal Democrat, Republican or Democratic foreign affairs positions, (and if you believe that you will believe anything!) no, this is not an anti-American poem either, for I love America and I love Americans, and I am a 2nd Amendment man myself as well. (Are you nervous yet!) No, this is a poem simply about what I see to be American, verbal political constipation. However, with the speedy rise of PC Manacles in the West, it will soon be outlawed to even say [viii] 'bollox' to the Queen.

My theory is that in Britain, where the long availability of toilets in public places still somewhat prevails, we much more freely and openly discuss our political aspirations and objections, and that whilst remaining friends! Our political system is a confrontational one, but at the end of the argument we can live together. With the influx of Islamic immigration, I am sure that will change. However, take 'Prime Minster's Question Time' for example, which is much better than Friday Night Smack Down and any cage fight you might want to watch, though [ix]Jeremy is trying to change that. When it's all said and done, the opposing parties love each other really! For now.

America (used to be) the land of freedom, however, God help you if your freedom of expression and understanding differs from someone else's political views! Especially the liberal leftists fascists Me thinks in America we need help to better publicly ruminate and remonstrate. You should contact your local congressman(person, sorry) insisting that Public Toilets are erected in every town square as soon as is convenient, if you'll excuse the pun. Too political? Well, just enjoy the poem and lighten up a little!.

PERFORMANCE TIPS |

With Po faced disappointment.

-----O-----

i You really need me to explain what a number two is?

ii Thomas Crapper was born in Yorkshire in 1836, into a family of modest means. At 14 years of age he was apprenticed to a Master Plumber in Chelsea, London. After serving his apprenticeship and then working as a journeyman, he set up in his own right in 1861 as a plumber in Robert Street, Chelsea. ... It is popularly thought that Mr. Crapper invented the W.C., and that the vulgar word for faeces is a derivative of his name, but neither belief is true. However, etymologists attest that the American word, "crapper", meaning the W.C. is directly from his name. He relentlessly promoted sanitary fittings to a somewhat dirty and sceptical world and championed the 'water-waste-preventing cistern syphon' in particular. Indeed, he invented the bathroom showroom and displayed his wares in large plate glass windows at the Marlboro' Works. This caused quite a stir and it is said that ladies observing the china bowls in the windows became faint at this shocking sight! (from Thomas-Crapper.com)

iii A French originated fully automated and self-cleaning toilet. When a user enters the toilet, the door closes to provide privacy. After the user has finished using the toilet, he exits and the door closes again. A wash cycle then begins inside the toilet, and the toilet fixture itself is scrubbed and disinfected automatically. After about sixty seconds, the toilet is again ready for use. Special Models are made for disabled people, and in Britain, in 2016, they are also used to house the homeless.

iv Like I say, the Superloo is an invention of the French Republic

v The Biblical Abraham, formerly Abram, though very rich, could not build or afford a Tank. The M1 Abrams, however, is an American third-generation main battle tank produced by the United States.

vi The Website 'InfoPlease' says, The Donkey— Presidential candidate Andrew Jackson was the first Democrat ever to be associated with the donkey symbol. His opponents during the election of 1828 tried to label him a "jackass" for his populist beliefs and slogan, "Let the people rule." Jackson was entertained by the notion and ended up using it to his advantage on his campaign posters. But cartoonist Thomas Nast is credited with making the donkey the recognized symbol of the Democratic Party. It first appeared in a cartoon in Harper's Weekly in 1870, and was supposed to represent an anti-Civil War faction. But the public was immediately taken by it and by 1880 it had already become the unofficial symbol of the party. Now, regarding the republican Elephant, it was political cartoonist Thomas Nast was also responsible for the Republican Party elephant. In a cartoon that appeared in Harper's Weekly in 1874, Nast drew a donkey clothed in lion's skin, scaring away all the animals at the zoo. One of those animals, the elephant, was labeled "The Republican Vote." That's all it took for the elephant to become associated with the Republican Party.

I wonder if Moses was a Republican that longed to be a Democrat? Or maybe a Theocratist that wished he was a Democrat, just so he could have someone to spread the blame of the nation upon?

vii I'm on a Wandering Biblical theme here. So, Moses, and the Moses I am referring to here is Charlton Heston, an American actor and right wing political activist. As a Hollywood star he appeared in 100 films over the course of 60 years and played Moses in the Ten Commandments. After being diagnosed with Alzheimer's disease in 2003, he retired from both acting and the National Rifle Association presidency. At the 2000 NRA convention, he raised a rifle over his head and declared that a potential Al Gore administration would take away his Second Amendment rights "from my cold, dead hands" He died in 2008. (This Poem was written whilst he was president of the NRA)

viii (Swing the lights and rub the salt off your shoulders) When I was in the Navy, this little saying was often repeated loudly in my ears by non-commissioned officers whenever I said anything wrong. "By the cringe Farrell," they would shout, "You'll be saying 'bollox' to the Queen next!" This was usually followed by colourful instructions regarding where to go and what to do when I finally arrived there.

ix Jeremy Corbyn. Just a bit more intelligent than Benny from Crossroads, and 2016 leader of the British Labour Party. Rag tag loony leftist, caught in a clothes explosion in an 'Age Concern' charity shop. The 1950's garments have never been able to be cut away from his sallow skin. When he retires, he is going to live in a communist colony in Rosyth which will occupy decommissioned Trident Submarines.

| 63-66 | VOL 01 | SUNSET BOULEVARD

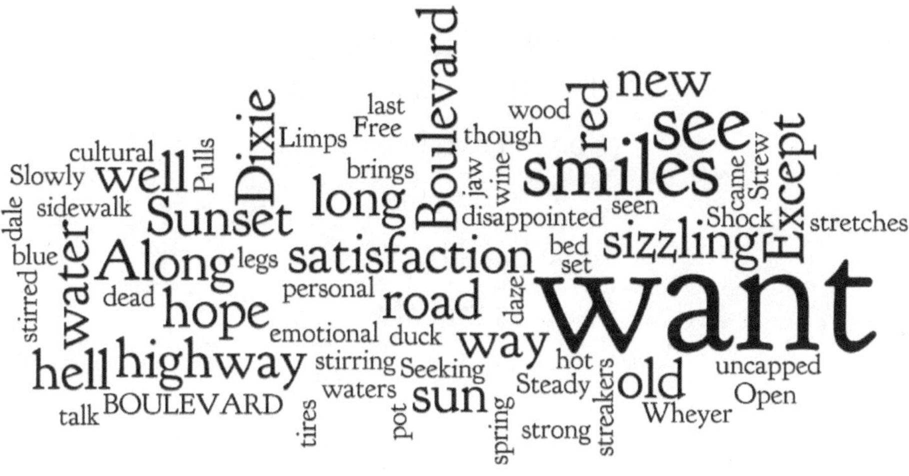

On Sunset Boulevard
Our [i]duck blue honey pot
Runs sticky in the sizzling sun
Soaking satisfaction
Smoking chicken on the dark wood decking
These new[ii] red necking streakers
Strew the sidewalk with their cultural clothes
And Scream through [iii]Bardstown
Happy in the hope that newness brings
For this road
Peach plump
Pregnant with possibility
Pulls cheeks wide
Nothing but smiles

Miles and miles of smiles
[iv]Wheyer?
Theyer!
Along the road of old
That stretches to Egypt
(So we have been told)
My!
What a by Way
Is this old
Dixie highway

He's been here since 77,
Sat in his chair, thinking of heaven
His stare
Slowly stupefied with a dead red wine
Is curious at these smiles
"What do they see?
I have sat here for years
[v]Waiting for an angel to stir the water
And man! I've been
Steady Eddy
Ever ready,
To take my leap of faith
Why, last time my waters stirred
I rolled this baby in
And out I came out with a new set of tires
It's true, don't knock it,

Life's like that, you don't always get what you want
Except it!
Crap happens
Except it!
Be happy with small miracles
Even though they mock you
Shock you
Sock you on the jaw
Show you the dower agin..

[vi]"Do you want to made well?"
"Well hell no of course not!
I love it here
I enjoy the emotional hassle
Of watching the lovely ladies
Leg their long strong limbs
Down [vii]Bonny Castle

Do I want to be well?
Free from my personal hell
Do I want to carry my bed and walk?
Open my mouth and talk
Stalk again
The deer of destiny
In the distant dale of dreams
Drink deep of the [viii]Dayspring from on High

Who's uncapped gusher
Shakes winter's spirit
Sprite spring green
Do I want to see?
Do I want to be seen?

Having no legs is a problem, but now my sight is gone
I no longer see the stirring of the water
Just the slaughter
Of my hope……
Along this by way
This dry way
This long hot Dixie highway"

On Sunset Boulevard
His disappointed daze
Limps sickly in the sizzling sun
Seeking satisfaction

-----O-----

PREAMBLE |

Now there is in Jerusalem by the Sheep Gate a pool, which is called in Hebrew, Bethesda, having five porches.3 In these lay a great multitude of sick people, blind, lame, paralyzed, waiting for the moving of the water.4 For an angel went down at a certain time into the pool and stirred up the water ; then whoever stepped in first, after the stirring of the water , was made well of whatever disease he had. (John 5:2-4 NKJV)

EXPLANATION |

On coming out of our 'dream apartment' in our new city, in a new country, we looked across the hot afternoon road to see a man of similar age sitting in his own wheelchair, on his own porch, with a very familiar glass of red wine in his hand. We talked. We felt guilty with our new hope, in this old, old place of his. One person's dreamland can be another person's prison; one person's heaven, another person's hell.

PERFORMANCE TIPS |

With hot sweaty and neck wiping confusion.

---

i This was the color of the house we were looking at, 'Duck Egg Blue' and it was indeed a sweet, sweet honey pot of a home! Actually I remember it being on 'Sunset something or other', somewhere in the Bonnie Castle area of the Highland of Louisville, Kentucky.

ii It was in the height of summer. I was wearing my unofficial seminary uniform of casual pants and a dress shirt. Yes indeed, the hot Kentucky sun had turned my neck bright red. I had a Farmer's tan!

iii Bardstown Road, in the Highlands of Louisville. Very eclectic in 2002 and always so overcome with a sense of its own uniqueness that it verged on silliness.

iv I love the Southern accent. Kentucky 'city talk' still inserts an extra syllable in every vowel even though they laugh at folks just twenty miles away from them that are still eating Squirrel brain sandwiches and shouting Yeeehaw!

vJohn 5:2-4

there is in Jerusalem by the Sheep Gate a pool, which is called in Hebrew, Bethesda, having five porches.

In these lay a great multitude of sick people, blind, lame, paralyzed, waiting for the moving of the water.

For an angel went down at a certain time into the pool and stirred up the water ; then whoever stepped in first, after the stirring of the water , was made well of whatever disease he had. NKJV

vi John 5:5-9 Now a certain man was there who had an infirmity thirty-eight years.

When Jesus saw him lying there, and knew that he already had been in that condition a long time, He said to him, "Do you want to be made well?"

The sick man answered Him, "Sir, I have no man to put me into the pool when the water is stirred up; but while I am coming, another steps down before me."

Jesus said to him, "Rise, take up your bed and walk."

And immediately the man was made well, took up his bed, and walked. And that day was the Sabbath. NKJV

vii Bonny Castle is both an area and a street name in the Highlands of Louisville Kentucky.

viii Luke 1:76-79

"And you, child, will be called the prophet of the Highest; For you will go before the face of the Lord to prepare His ways,

To give knowledge of salvation to His people By the remission of their sins,

Through the tender mercy of our God, With which the Dayspring from on high has visited us;

To give light to those who sit in darkness and the shadow of death, To guide our feet into the way of peace." NKJV

| 64-66 | VOL 01 | HERE COMES THE PEELER

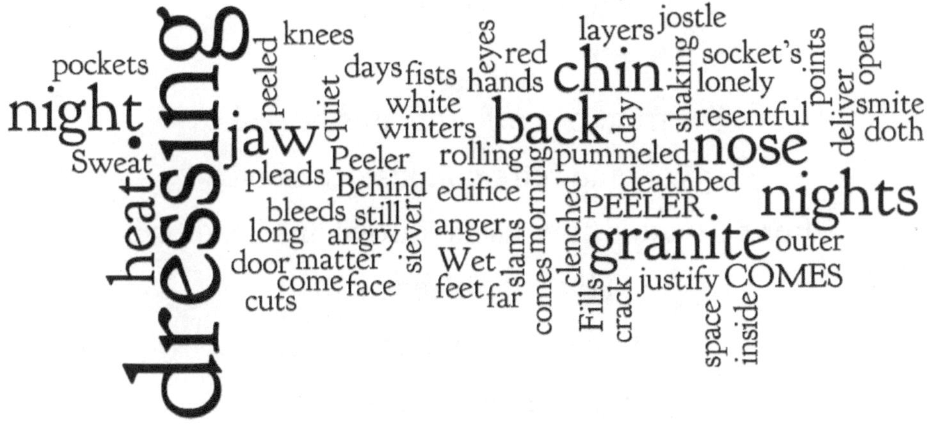

[i]

He cuts his nose to smite his face
[ii]And points his chin to outer space
With granite jaw
He slams the door
Behind his stomping feet, and
His fists clenched heat,
Sweat his palms inside his pummeled pockets
And the white of winters snows
Fills the socket's of his blinded eyes rolling back
As he angry goes into the [iii]crack of night
And into the night he creeps,

Here comes the [iv]Peeler

The siever of our woes
To tease away the layers of our days
And expose them to the loneliness of all our
Long, cold nights.

[v]So, from resentful dreams he wakes
Wet and red upon his deathbed
For no matter how far he throws his head back
His nose bleeds still
His jelly chin doth quiver
His granite jaw no more
The stony edifice of morning
Now long gone
As his now open hands
Hang between his shaking knees and
He pleads for the jostle of the day
To come and justify his dressing,
His dressing up in lonely anger,
[vi]His dressing down in deep regret

What a dressing down our heat peeled hearts deliver us
In the quiet of our nights.

Let all bitterness, wrath, anger, clamour, and evil speaking be put away from you, with all malice. And be kind to one another, tender hearted, forgiving one another, just as God in Christ forgave you. (Eph 4:31-32 NKJV)

EXPLANATION |

Anger works well in self-justifying madness if it is both loud and demonstrative. However, the quiet will always inevitably follow the storm, when we are alone, uncontrollably video vomiting the events before the eyes of our imagination, constantly regurgitating, always regretting, and wishing for a repenting. The self-harm of anger is profound and lasts for years. The policeman of God, the conscience, if he is still alive, will always come and convict us of our misdemeanors. Always. Be thankful for the 'dressing down' this policeman of God gives you when he comes knocking on your door and gets you out of bed in the middle of the night.

PERFORMANCE TIPS |

This is a poem of contrasts. The commentator looking onto the regretful scene reflects the anger of the Mussolini madness in fast speaking and visual action as the furious object of his contemplation is leaving the room. There are subtle allusions here to drug taking in the form of the word emphasis of 'crack' and associated nose bleeds. If you can do some sniffing around these words, maybe even before you begin the piece, then maybe your listeners will see the scene in more defined detail.The Poem slows down and hinges in that little phrase 'Here comes The Peeler.' The piece ends with a cutting comment, it is open ended, drawing the listener to a mental agreement with the observation of the commentator. That's all. If there is any more to be done, let the policeman do it.

-----O-----

i This is an interesting 16th Century English saying which means - "To Disadvantage yourself, even hurtfully so, in order to do harm to an enemy or adversary."

ii This is the Mussolini madness I refer to. It is nothing short of hands of the hips bare-face pride.

iii Crack Cocaine can of course be smoked. It has been my observation that drug use fosters a paranoia playing field where prideful anger likes to go out to play. There is no darker night that a drug induced play of pride and anger, that can break relationships for years. Highs of anger, dilated pupils will all lead to vertigo and then down you'll go to the low, low, low.

iv Peelers are the old fashioned named given to Policemen. You know, Bobbies, named after their founder, Sir Robert Peel, former Conservative prime minister of 1834. Our conscience is the Policeman, the Sheriff of God.

v Conscience has its voice in the conscious mind and the subconscious. In our open eyed visitations and the hauntings of our dreams. As long as he is alive and free, then Conscience will be heard!

vi Conscience is there not just to condemn us, but to point us in a better direction, it is there to take us to the teacher. It dresses us down for sure, but for a purpose. You see, 'to dress' someone is an old expression for 'to punish' them. To be dressed down is a nautical expression used for sails that became old and could not hold the wind. When that happened, they were 'dressed down. That is. taken down and re-dressed with oil and wax, to make them hold the wind again. So, a sailor who was 'dressed down' was treated in a way which would, hopefully, dramatically improve his effectiveness. We have forgotten that unfortunately and so these days the term mostly means to give someone a 'very harsh talking to.'

| 65-66 | VOL 01 | BEDTIME

Days end and
Dusk lays its cloudy darkened duvet
Fringed with sun-set silver
Across the
Warm
Wet
Earth

So that mourning
Shall again give birth

To singing gladness

-----O-----

PREAMBLE |

Weeping may endure for a night, But joy comes in the morning.(Ps 30:5 NKJV)

EXPLANATION |

It's good to go to bed and remember the goodness of the day and bathe them in the expectations of the morrow.

PERFORMANCE TIPS |

With satisfied tiredness and happy expectancy.

-----O-----

| 66-66 | VOL 01 | LOVE'S GREEN EYES

As strong as death
No, stronger still
And so my Lord
My foes would kill
To sin, self, world
And all false thing
No mercy shows
My jealous King

Cruel as the grave
His broken heart
Weeps for the loss
Of this poor tart
And for my heart

An offering
The death of Christ
My Jealous King

His arms tattooed
With my new name
A blazing fire
A mighty flame
None of the seas
Could ever douse
No wealth redeem
My feeble house

As strong as death
Cruel as the grave
Through loves green grasp
My Lord did save
This rebel son
This excrement

So He could be pre-eminent

-----O-----

PREAMBLE |

Set me as a seal upon your heart, As a seal upon your arm; For love is as strong as death, Jealousy as cruel as the grave; Its flames are flames of fire, A most vehement flame. Many waters cannot quench

love, Nor can the floods drown it. If a man would give for love All the wealth of his house, It would be utterly despised. (Song 8:6-7 NKJV)

EXPLANATION |

Here's an untouched truth; The good that lies in Jealousy! Or maybe, the God that lies in Jealousy

Dear friends, I hope so much these poems have at least pointed to the great struggle of our flesh with God the Holy Spirit, that is, the lifting up and pre-eminence of Christ in us redeemed pots of clay. God is merciful and loving, let all God's people say "AMEN" and let us remember that each day, not as an excuse to continue in sin, but as a means to become more than conquerors over sin; our sin, your sin, my sin. Amen and let it be so.

PERFORMANCE TIPS |

With pride!

-----O-----

Our Sponsors | Poetry.Coffee

Purple Robert

is pleased and proud to be sponsored by

Poetry.Coffee

The Voice of The Bean

Providing unique flavor coffee tones both to Poets and Poetry groups throughout the world!

Great Gifts

Great Prices

Great Coffee

Find out how your poetry group can get hold of Poetry.Coffee email | sales@Poetry.Coffee

Do you want to be a Purple Poet?

The you can join the us www.PurplePoets.Net today!

Member benefits include

1. Being part of a growing 'Purple Poetry Network' of 'The Purple Poets Club!' in your area. We are chiefly 'Performance Poets,' but also writers, novelists, and self-employed publishers, all with a shed load of experience and creativity. Most of all, we help each other.
2. Resources and assistance in setting up and maintaining and growing a 'Purple Poets Club' in your area.
3. Free access to all 'Purple Poets Club' competitions.
4. Discounted rates for you and your 'Purple Poets Club' from all related products sold at Poetry.Coffee
5. Advice on publication and promotion of your own poetic works.
6. More than all of this though, we really do care about you and want you to discover your own unique voice! Remember, we are different. We are family.

So, if you want to join or even start a local 'Purple Poetry Club,'

go directly to

www.ThePurplePoets.Club

Purple Robert Volume 01 thru Volume 07

Did you know there are **7** Volumes of **66Poems**?

1. **Volume 01 of 07** ***Mrs. Sharwood is My Concubine***
2. **Volume 02 of 07** ***Mrs. Dalrymple's Pimple***
3. **Volume 03 of 07** ***Lovers of the Blood Stained Page***
4. **Volume 04 of 07** ***The Reluctant Tinker***
5. **Volume 05 of 07** ***The Dove on Distant Oaks***
6. **Volume 06 of 07** ***The Undiscovered Country***
7. **Volume 07 of 07** ***Crown Lands***

You can order your next available copy of
66Poems today from,

www.whisperingword.com

Have you heard of Night-Whispers?

If you liked the Meta-Physical aspects of Purple Robert then you might just love his 'Everyday Bible Insights' called Night-Whispers. Maybe you need to order a copy?To do this today, simply go to

www.NightWhispers.com

---------------------------0---------------------------

Night-Whispers is written by Victor Robert Farrell, produced by WhisperingWord Ltd. and licenced for the sole use of, The 66 Books Ministry A modern day, Back to the whole Bible, Boots on The Ground, Proclamation Movement. www.66Books.tv

THE MISSION STATEMENT OF THE 66 BOOKS MINISTRY

WWW.66Books.tv | Our Mission is:

1. "To proclaim Jesus, the Savior of the whole world, from the whole Bible, because He is wonderful!"

2. Indeed, we are constrained by the love of God, to communicate the rawness of the Bible to real people, in real ways, and our driving and major project of '66Cities' shall take us to the 66 most influential cities of the 250 nations of the world in the next 25 years. That's 16,500 cities!

3. We are aiming to build relationships with grass roots, real people, that is, ordinary people, who, in their own countries and cities, want to do extraordinary things for Jesus and the Kingdom of God, to bring a Biblical Gospel message that is relevant to now, in a world that has come to believe that Jesus is irrelevant to their lives.

If you would like to partner with us in this great task. Then we want to hear from you! Contact me today on vr@66books.tv

MORE ABOUT 'THE 66 BOOKS MINISTRY'

WWW.66Cities.com | By the year 2047, by the grace of God and according to His will and favor, The 66 Books Ministry shall be preaching consecutively from each of the 66 Books of the Holy Bible, the Gospel of the Lord Jesus Christ in 16,500 of the most influential cities of the world on an annual and ongoing basis!

We do not underestimate the quality teams of trained people that this will take, together with the need for vast amount of materials and finances which will also have to be raised. However, as most futurists indicate that the growing global population will be gathered mostly in major world cities in the coming years, there is a necessity laid upon the church to present and proclaim the God of the whole Bible, through the primacy of preaching in these cities. We are convinced that this is a paramount and pressing concern.

"For since, in the wisdom of God, the world through wisdom did not know God, it pleased God through the foolishness of the message preached to save those who believe" 1 Corinthians 1:21NKJV

"Preach the Word! Be ready in season and out of season. Convince, rebuke, exhort, with all longsuffering and teaching." 2 Timothy 4:2NKJV

The church is looking for a revival. The 66 Books Ministry, however, is trying to start a revolution of a return to the preached Word, from the whole of the Bible as a precursor to any and all coming revival.

For "whoever calls on the name of the Lord shall be saved." How then shall they call on Him in whom they have not believed? And how shall they believe in Him of whom they have not heard? And how shall they hear without a preacher? And how shall they preach unless they are sent? As it is written: "How beautiful are the feet of those who preach the gospel of peace, Who bring glad tidings of good things!" Romans 10:13-15 NKJV

We are unashamedly looking for and seeking to foster a massive, huge, releasing, transformative, and exceptionally disruptive reversal and revolutionary change, both within the church and then in the world. We are not just another mission trying to do the same as every other mission. We are intent on revolution!

To this revolutionary end, we have no fear of seeming failure and will cultivate that audacious atmosphere within our ministry. We want to attract grass roots people who are people of faith risk takers, for we believe it is people of such life hazarding attitudes that are used by God to make breakthroughs in the world for the Kingdom of God. Hanging back for fear of seeming failure, hanging back and waiting for the trained professionals, both wastes the time of the church time and kills the spirit of victory.

In that spirit then, we therefore are believing that this task can be accomplished by such people within the time frame we have given ourselves.

Fully assured then, that we are in full obedience with the great commission of our great God and Savior Jesus Christ, we do, with great confidence in Him, turn ourselves happily to this so great a task in the hope that, like a happy hound straining at the leash to be let loose, we believe that many other people will smile along with us and be part of this brand new grass roots 21st Century Global City Mission.

If you want to know more and want to be part of what we are doing then go to www.The66BooksMinistry.com or call us in the USA on **855 662 6657**, or email V.R. directly on vr@66Books.TV

AUTHOR BIO | PURPLE ROBERT

It won't take too much investigation for you to find out that Purple Robert is in fact, Victor Robert Farrell (Born 1960 and alive until now and still kicking) was born in Chesterfield England to Scottish parents with Irish grandparents, which is an obvious recipe both for writing and emotional disaster if ever there was one!

He grew up a culturally excluded Roman Catholic (his parents were divorced,) which is one of the reasons why he hates religion with a passion, and that's an interesting enough fact by itself, because he is also an ordained protestant minister to boot.

Purple Robert. became a Christian whilst serving on board a Polaris Submarine at the end of the cold war. He has gone on to do many things, including being a broadcaster, App developer, performance poet, and the long-time author of 'Night Whispers,' which is read in over 100 counties and is also translated into Spanish (see www.Night Whispers.com)

Currently, Purple Robert is also President of The 66 Books Ministry: a grass roots global city mission endeavor. I suppose it is this concoction of background and experience which means Purple Robert's communication is always raw and emotive. After all, and as he says, *"If Christianity can be relevant on a Monday morning, several hundred feet underneath an unknown ocean, in a pornographic sewer pipe carrying enough nuclear weapons to destroy a continent whilst hiding from the Russians, then it can be relevant anywhere and everywhere!"*

Purple Robert sees himself as a servant of the 'Word of the Lord' to tasked communicate the God of the whole Bible. His proclamation of the same is done in very raw terms to very real people, is both his burden and his passion.

| May 26th | Reading 147 of 366 |

MORNING → | HISTORICAL BOOKS

BOOK 11 of 66 → | 1 KINGS 16,17

Signpost Words → | 'AN ANSWER'

Highlight Verses → | 1 Kings 16:31-34

And it came to pass, as though it had been a trivial thing for him to walk in the sins of Jeroboam the son of Nebat, that he took as wife Jezebel the daughter of Ethbaal, king of the Sidonians; and he went and served Baal and worshiped him. Then he set up an altar for Baal in the temple of Baal, which he had built in Samaria. And Ahab made a wooden image. Ahab did more to provoke the Lord God of Israel to anger than all the kings of Israel who were before him. In his days Hiel of Bethel built Jericho. He laid its foundation with Abiram his firstborn, and with his youngest son Segub he set up its gates, according to the word of the Lord, which He had spoken through Joshua the son of Nun. NKJV

Some Observations → |

This is nothing but an extended killing time, and it is God who is slaughtering His wayward nation. Decade after decade the decadent mobster kings steer the people more and more out of the way of the Lord. Dogs lick up the blood from slaughtered corpses, birds peck the watery eyeballs out of the maggot eaten heads. Death and destruction stalk the land, yet still the people rise up to pray to an idle and engage in sexual sin. The mercy of God is seen on two legs and heard from one mouth, even the prophets of the Lord. Now, dropped from heaven, out of nowhere, in answer to the madness of Ahab the loon, a prophet like no other arrives on the scene. Elijah the Tishbite

A Call To Action → |

Fine pulpits and finer churches, are rarely the abode of the prophet.

EVENING → | PAULINE EPISTLES

BOOK 46 of 66 → | 1 CORINTHIANS 15

Signpost Words → | 'ASSURANCE OF SALVATION'

Highlight Verses → | 1 Corinthians 15:1-11

Moreover, brethren, I declare to you the gospel which I preached to you, which also you received and in which you stand, by which also you are saved, if you hold fast that word which I preached to you— unless you believed in vain. For I delivered to you first of all that which I also received: that Christ died for our sins according to the Scriptures, and that He was buried, and that He rose again the third day according to the Scriptures, and that He was seen by Cephas, then by the twelve. After that He was seen by over five hundred brethren at once, of whom the greater part remain to the present, but some have fallen asleep. After that He was seen by James, then by all the apostles. Then last of all He was seen by me also, as by one born out of due time. For I am the least of the apostles, who am not worthy to be called an apostle, because I persecuted the church of God. But by the grace of God I am what I am, and His grace toward me was not in vain; but I labored more abundantly than they all, yet not I, but the grace of God which was with me.... NKJV

Some Observations → |

The two 'wee' words we Evangelicals dislike to discourse upon are 'if' and 'unless.' I believe that once we are saved we are always saved, 'IF' we continue on receiving, believing and standing. I believe that once we are saved we are always saved, 'UNLESS' we prove ourselves to be unfaithful and reprobate in forsaking the Christ of the Scriptures. Paul did not believe he was saved by our works, yet by grace he worked his little heine off!

A Call To Action → |

Continuance in the work of grace is the key to your own assurance.

JOIN THE FELLOWSHIP OF THE BOOK

WWW.TheFellowShipofTheBook.com

The Fellowship of The Book is a Daily Bible Reading Fellowship. It is a morning and evening devotional of four books available each quarter of the year. It includes

Signpost Words
Highlight Verses
Some Observations
Call To Action

Consecutively, Chronologically and in many other ways, Read The Bible Thru in 1 just one year, with both Morning and Evening reading to keep your mind focused on the Lord of the Word and the Word of The Lord. Buy this and several other ways to 'Read the Bible Thru in a Year Books' at www.whisperingword.com

ANOTHER BOOK BY THE AUTHOR, VR

Habakkuk A Prophecy For Our Time

As the Church in the West is found to be mostly dead and covered with Laodicean lukewarm vomit, as The Lord, slips the dead things silently over the side of the storm tossed ship into the dark oblivion of the waves of secular humanism and rising Islam, what remains will need to be fortified with steel to live in a quickly changing anti-Christian world of persecution. There is no better prophecy more equipped to speak to such a remnant who shall be so very besieged. Welcome to Habakkuk, 35 of 66, a prophecy for our time.

Buy at www.whisperingword.com

ANOTHER BOOK BY THE AUTHOR, VR

The 66-Minute Bible

I am told that there are 788,258 words in the King James Bible and of these 14,565 are unique. That's a lot of words! I have been reading the Bible for nearly forty years on an almost daily basis. It still remains to me the most exciting book on the planet, however, it never gets any easier. Bible reading is a spiritual discipline and for me the emphasis is on discipline. I created this resource to aid you in your Bible reading, it gives your brain a sixty second overview of the Bible, a loose enclosure to herd the narrative of the book into something that can be seen as a whole. It was never created to be a substitute, but an aid. Just saying...... Friends, welcome to the most exciting book on the planet! V.R.

Buy at www.whisperingword.com

www.ingramcontent.com/pod-product-compliance
Lightning Source LLC
LaVergne TN
LVHW040825090826
845145LV00001BA/205

* 9 7 8 1 9 1 0 6 8 6 8 8 1 *